The College, the Constitution, and the Consumer Student:
Implications for Policy and Practice

by Robert M. Hendrickson and Annette Gibbs

ASHE-ERIC Higher Education Report No. 7, 1986

Prepared by

Clearinghouse on Higher Education
The George Washington University

Published by

Association for the Study of Higher Education

Jonathan D. Fife,
Series Editor

Cite as
Hendrickson, Robert M., and Gibbs, Annette. *The College, the Constitution, and the Consumer Student: Implications for Policy and Practice* ASHE-ERIC Higher Education Report No. 7. Washington, D.C.: Association for the Study of Higher Education, 1986.

Cover design by Michael David Brown, Inc., Rockville, MD.

The ERIC Clearinghouse on Higher Education invites individuals to submit proposals for writing monographs for the Higher Education Report series. Proposals must include:
1. A detailed manuscript proposal of not more than five pages.
2. A 75-word summary to be used by several review committees for the initial screening and rating of each proposal.
3. A vita.
4. A writing sample.

Library of Congress Catalog Card Number 86-70536
ISSN 0884-0040
ISBN 0-913317-34-9

ERIC° **Clearinghouse on Higher Education**
The George Washington University
One Dupont Circle, Suite 630
Washington, D.C. 20036

ASHE Association for the Study of Higher Education
One Dupont Circle, Suite 630
Washington, D.C. 20036

OERI
Office of Educational Research and Improvement
U.S. Department of Education

This publication was partially prepared with funding from the Office of Educational Research and Improvement, U.S. Department of Education, under contract no. 400-86-0017. The opinions expressed in this report do not necessarily reflect the positions or policies of OERI or the Department.

EXECUTIVE SUMMARY

The relationship between student and college is at the heart
of collegiate education. At one time, the relationship was
largely taken for granted or subsumed under a nonspecific
notion of in loco parentis in which the college was the principal determiner of the educational environment. Since
1960, however, this relationship has changed, and today
these multifaceted relationships, described as fiduciary,
contractual, and constitutional, take the form of rights
defined by the Constitution or by the student as consumer.

Litigation involving the constitutional relationship has
moved from an emphasis on individual rights in the 1960s
and 1970s to First Amendment rights of association and
freedom of religion as they affect student organizations in
the late 1970s and 1980s. Another First Amendment
issue—commercial speech—has also been defined during
the last several years.

Issues involving contractual and fiduciary relationships
have been litigated as torts based on negligence, breach of
contract, or educational malpractice. The novel consumer
litigation lies in the area of educational malpractice, and
adequate litigation exists to plot some future directions and
trends. Consumer protection has become more important
than in the past, and colleges find themselves struggling to
design policies that are both consumer focused and preserve past policies appropriate for their primary mission.

What Rights Do Student Organizations Have on Campus?
Administrators of public colleges and universities are
bound by the First and Fourteenth Amendments to ensure
that rights and privileges are extended to *all* student groups
equally and fairly. Administrators of private colleges, while
not bound legally by constitutional considerations, may
find less conflict acknowledging rights and freedoms
required of public colleges by the Constitution, particularly
at this time, when American society places a great deal of
importance on those rights.

While speech-related activities of student organizations
are constitutionally protected, they are subject, however,
to some regulation as a result of the special characteristics
of the school environment. In balancing the constitutional
rights of students and the prerogatives of the institution,
administrators must ensure that:

- Freedom of *speech* is guaranteed, but *behavior* is subject to regulation.
- Behavior that interferes with or disrupts the normal activities of the institution or the rights of others is subject to regulation.
- Regulation of time, place, and manner is lawful for maintaining the proper educational environment of the college or university.
- Once some groups or organizations have been recognized by the institution, *all* groups must be accorded such status, provided they meet the same lawful procedural and substantive requirements.
- Religious speech must be treated as secular speech as it relates to recognition of student organizations and policies regarding the use of institutional facilities.

What Issues Surround the Collection and Allocation of Mandatory Student Activity Fees?
Major legal challenges to mandatory student fees have alleged that certain uses of the fees violate students' constitutionally protected rights to freedom of religion or freedoms to associate, speak, and express themselves. In both areas, the courts have deferred to administrative discretion, balancing the interests of colleges and universities in the use of the fees against students' First Amendment rights.

College administrators should thus structure fee systems to ensure the presence of as many of the following characteristics as possible:

- The group receiving funds is an institutionally dependent, on-campus organization.
- The primary purpose or activity of the group receiving funds is educational—not political—and the group permits expression of a wide range of views.
- The funding mechanism is one to which all on-campus groups have equal access.
- The fee system allows a maximum amount of discussion, approval, or objection by students at the outset, before fees are ever exacted.
- The institutional student activity fee must support a broad forum of ideas and activities, while not promoting or hindering expression of any particular view.

It is unlikely that an absence of any one of these characteristics will make a mandatory fee system stand or fall. Absent clear direction from the courts on the issue and a controlling Supreme Court decision, however, implementation of a fee system with as many of these guidelines as possible is likely to be the best course for avoiding legitimate disruptive student dissent and costly, time-consuming litigation.

What Rights Do Vendors Have on Campus?
The First Amendment's freedom of speech is not absolute. To ensure the implementation of free expression, the Supreme Court has determined that restrictions regarding time, place, and manner of individual expression must satisfy four requirements: They must (1) be content neutral and (2) narrowly drawn, (3) serve a significant governmental interest, and (4) leave open alternative channels of communication. Commercial solicitation, as a form of commercial speech, is afforded less than the full array of constitutional safeguards for free speech.

The courts have ruled further that:

- Administrators may ban group commercial solicitation in students' residence hall rooms.
- College officials are well advised to prevent the use of residence hall rooms as merchandising marts by commercial vendors.
- A one-on-one demonstration and/or sale in a student's private room may be allowed *if the student invites the solicitor.*
- Institutions should provide some means for allowing commercial speech, information, and expression, including newspapers, mail, radio stations, and telephone, for example.
- Colleges and universities may prohibit any misleading or unlawful commercial activity.

What Is the Status of Educational Malpractice?
The current disposition of the courts is not to encroach into some areas of the fiduciary relationship—specifically academic decision making—which includes, for the moment, educational malpractice. The courts refuse to recognize educational malpractice as a tort, because to do so

would conflict with public policy. This position is consistent with the case law on academic dismissal.

Several policy considerations seem appropriate.

- The process for peer review and evaluation by department heads and supervisory administrators should be reviewed to ensure that incompetence and poor performance are not swept under the rug.
- Institutions should ensure that diagnostic procedures meet the practices and procedures accepted by professionals in the field when such standards are available.
- Review should be built into the process of awarding grades and certifying skills to protect against arbitrary and capricious decisions and, at the same time, to protect the academic integrity of the faculty evaluation process.
- Catalogs, bulletins, and other publications should be reviewed to ensure that they do not make guarantees beyond the institution's capabilities.

While this monograph provides information essential to the development of educational policy, it is not a substitute for the advice of legal counsel.

ADVISORY BOARD

CONSULTING EDITORS

Paul A. Albrecht
Executive Vice President and Dean
Claremont Graduate School

G. Lester Anderson
Professor Emeritus
Pennsylvania State University

Robert C. Andringa
President
Creative Solutions

John B. Bennett
Director
Office on Self-Regulation
American Council on Education

Carole J. Bland
Associate Professor
Department of Family Practice and Community Health
University of Minnesota

Judith A. Clementson-Mohr
Director of Psychological Services
Purdue University

Mark H. Curtis
President Emeritus
Association of American Colleges

Martin Finkelstein
Associate Professor of Higher Education Administration
Seton Hall University

Andrew T. Ford
Provost and Dean of College
Allegheny College

Roderick S. French
Vice President for Academic Affairs
George Washington University

Timothy Gallineau
Vice President for Student Development
Saint Bonaventure University

G. Manuel Gunne
Adjunct Associate Professor
College of Nursing
University of Utah

CONTENTS

FOREWORD

The most significant change in the relationship between students and higher education institutions occurred in the late 1960s and early 1970s when the states lowered the age of majority from 21 to 18. As a result, most college students are considered adults in terms of legal status, rights, and responsibilities. Colleges no longer are parental stand-ins, subject to the protection that that special status implies; they are now more like commercial enterprises offering contractual services.

The revised status of college students is also reflected in the court's recognition of their constitutional rights. While particularly applicable to public institutions, this new emphasis reflects changing societal values that most private institutions should also find advisable to consider. Perhaps the most significant change in the relationship between students and their colleges is that institutions no longer can assume, given their special status as educational entities, that they are immune from possible litigation. While it is still true that the courts will give colleges and universities deference in academic matters, they are holding institutions accountable for failing to provide agreed on services and administrative procedures.

The 1980s have seen an increased tendency for litigation. Administrative awareness of individual rights and institutional responsibilities can minimize the possibility of the assessment of damages. Certainly, the possibility of being sued should be kept in mind when developing policies and procedures governing student activities.

In this report, Robert Hendrickson, professor-in-charge of the Higher Education Program at the Pennsylvania State University, and Annette Gibbs, professor in the Center for the Study of Higher Education at the University of Virginia, have reviewed and analyzed recent legal developments concerning students and their institutions. The authors have concentrated on constitutional issues related to the rights of students to organize, the collection and allocation of mandatory student activity fees, and the protection of freedom of speech regarding commercial enterprises. Concluding with a discussion of academic malpractice, the authors offer suggestions for policy development.

Administrators, especially student personnel administrators, can benefit greatly from this report as they develop policy and procedures guiding their relationship with students. Given the nature of legal issues and their propensity to change direction rapidly, administrators will find this book a valuable reference work.

ACKNOWLEDGMENTS

The authors wish to acknowledge the research conducted by James J. Szablewicz, a student at the School of Law, The University of Virginia, and Morgan M. Laury, a doctoral student in higher education, The Pennsylvania State University. Thanks are also expressed to Margaret A. Sutherland for preparing the manuscript and to Janet C. Shank for editing and preparing the final copy of the manuscript.

STUDENT-INSTITUTIONAL RELATIONSHIPS

The relationship between student and college is at the heart of collegiate education. At one time, the relationship was largely taken for granted or subsumed under a nonspecific notion of in loco parentis in which the college was the principal determiner of the educational environment. Since 1960, however, this relationship has changed, and today these multifaceted relationships take the form of rights defined by the Constitution or by the student as consumer.

Dixon is credited with changing the student-institutional relationship from one of in loco parentis to . . . one based on the Constitution.

The student-institutional relationship has received considerable attention in the literature since *Dixon* v. *Alabama* [294 F.2d 150 (5th Cir. 1961); *cert. denied,* 286 U.S. 930 (1961)], which requires public institutions to give due process to students in disciplinary dismissal cases. *Dixon* is credited with changing the student-institutional relationship from one of in loco parentis to a new one based on the Constitution. One of the first constitutional law scholars to propose this new relationship suggested that in loco parentis was no longer a viable way to conceptualize the relationship between students and the institution and that constitutional parameters were now in control of some aspects of it (Van Alstyne 1962, 1965, 1968a, 1968b).

While some announced the death of in loco parentis (Young 1973), others saw it as having a minimal influence in describing the student-institutional relationship (Chambers 1976; Diener 1971). More recently, the literature reflects multiple, situation-specific relationships, and the courts are still discussing a special relationship between student and institution that is similar to the concept of in loco parentis (Conrath 1976). At the same time, the literature and court cases reflect a more sophisticated view of the student as consumer that in legal theory substitutes contractual and fiduciary relationships for in loco parentis. And the constitutional relationship has been evolving. While post-*Dixon* decisions focused on students' rights—due process, privacy, freedom of speech and association—more recent pivotal decisions have involved rights of student *groups,* particularly as they relate to the First Amendment. This new case law and the liability and malpractice litigation affecting the fiduciary relationship in the last few years form the novel case law giving rise to this monograph.

In Loco Parentis
Interest in in loco parentis peaked in the late 1960s and early 1970s, when a number of studies found support for

the existence of the concept in higher education institutions (Johnson 1971; Serra 1968; Wagoner 1968). Much of the literature on legal issues published during that period reflects the debate about in loco parentis as a viable practical and legal concept, and as late as 1976, one study found the doctrine of in loco parentis continuing to describe the relationship between student and institution (Conrath 1976).

In loco parentis as a legal concept can be traced back to English common law (Harms 1970) and early case law. One of the most frequently cited cases in the literature, *Gott* v. *Berea College* [161 S.W. 204 (Ky. 1913)], states:

> *College authorities stand* in loco parentis *concerning the physical and moral welfare and mental training of pupils, and we are unable to see why, to that end, they may not make any rules or regulations for the government or betterment of their pupils that a parent could for the same purpose* (p. 206).

Anthoney v. *Syracuse University* [231 N.Y.S. 435 (N.Y. App. Div. 1928)] further emphasizes the complete authority the institution has over students. In that case, a female student was dismissed because she was not a "typical Syracuse girl," and the institution was given unlimited authority to determine the nature of its relationship with students (Kaplin 1979, p. 6).

A more recent case, *Evans* v. *State Board of Agriculture* [325 F. Supp. 1353 (E.D. Colo. 1971)], indicates continuing support of in loco parentis under certain circumstances, assuming the existence of in loco parentis as the legal basis for the institutional authority to make and enforce rules that control the campus environment and make it conducive to the pursuit of learning (Conrath 1976, p. 139). But even though the concept of in loco parentis no longer adequately explains the student-institutional relationship, especially when considering students' rights [see *Buttney* v. *Smiley*, 281 F. Supp. 280 (D. Colo. 1968); *Moore* v. *Student Affairs Committee of Troy State University*, 284 F. Supp. 725 (M.D. Ala. 1968)], dicta in these cases still indicate a reluctance to totally disregard the concept (Conrath 1976, pp. 173, 175).

The literature reflects the continuing existence of in loco parentis as a student-institutional relationship, but in terms of the legal implications, it is more appropriate to view it in terms of the fiduciary relationship.

Fiduciary Relationship
A fiduciary relationship:

> . . . exists where there is special confidence reposed in one who in equity and good conscience is bound to act in good faith with due regard to the interests of the one reposing the confidence (Black 1979, p. 753).

This relationship—the "trust theory" (Alexander and Solomon 1972, p. 413)—is one in which the institution possesses the knowledge to determine not only what is necessary to produce an educated individual but also the environment most conducive to learning (see Diener 1971; Lerblance 1979). The fact that the court gives deference to academicians in academic dismissal cases, as it did in *Board of Curators of the University of Missouri* v. *Horowitz* [435 U.S. 78 (1978)], lends further credence to the existence of the fiduciary relationship. (Academic deference, discussed in detail later, explains the court's reluctance to focus on the fiduciary relationship.)

The fiduciary relationship defines the relationship between a patient and a client. Educators have that same patient-to-client relationship inside and outside the classroom. Students place trust in the institution and its staff to deliver educational programs that will improve their capabilities as functioning adults. The existence of licensing procedures for higher education institutions is a state mechanism to protect the public against fraudulent institutions, and it is similar to the licensing practices in other professions where a fiduciary relationship is present. The fiduciary relationship is important in the developing legal concept of educational malpractice and is closely related to contract theory.

Contract Theory
Contract theory has been recognized as one student-institutional relationship. The most frequently cited case in which contract theory has its origins in case law is *Carr* v. *St. Johns University* [231 N.Y.S.2d 403 (N.Y. App. Div. 1962); aff'd, 235 N.Y.S.2d 834 (N.Y. 1962)], which recog-

nized contractual relationships that go beyond expressed contracts between students and the institution. An implied contract at a private university, for example, was used to support the dismissal of a student for failing "to comply with the university's prescribed terms" (Kaplin 1979, p. 178). A subsequent case, *Healy* v. *Larsson* [323 N.Y.S.2d 625 (N.Y. Sup. Ct. 1971); *aff'd,* 348 N.Y.S.2d 971 (N.Y. App. Div. 1971); *aff'd,* 360 N.Y.S.2d 419 (N.Y. 1974)], extended the enforcement of similar contractual relationships to public universities: An institution was forced to award a degree to a student who had satisfactorily completed the degree requirements prescribed by an academic counselor during his attendance (Kaplin 1979, p. 179). The counselor's advice was viewed as an implied contract.

The interpretation of the courts' adherence to certain contract principles will be important in determining the direction contract theory takes (Kaplin 1979, p. 181). For example, the courts do not usually enforce "unconscionable contracts" (contracts that unfairly favor the stronger party to the detriment of the other and would be unacceptable to the reasonable person without coercion), and "contracts of adhesion . . . offered on a 'take it or leave it' basis, with no opportunity to negotiate the terms," may also tip the courts' favor toward the weaker party when controversy or ambiguities exist (p. 182). Both legal principles may be significant, not only in questions of liability but also in the area of educational malpractice, as they involve a relationship between institution and student that is similar to the fiduciary relationship.

Institutions should carefully review policies and practices affecting students to be sure that they are free of "language suggestive of commitment (or promise) to students" (p. 182). Not only should an institution be aware of what it is promising; it should also eliminate promises it is unable to deliver.

This question of fair practice in higher education is addressed in literature setting out a code of fair practice (El-Khawas 1979). Similarly, the new consumerism, while focusing on an issue that arises out of federal regulations, also has a basis in contract theory (Stark 1976). A "contract to educate," which finds its origins in college bulletins and other publications, is recommended as a conceptual framework for use by the courts to define the student-institutional relationship (Nordin 1982). These publications tie the contractual relationship to consumer protection and educational malpractice in higher education (see Bean and Hines 1981). Questions surrounding liability and educational malpractice and the student as consumer have been addressed in numerous litigations.

Constitutional Relationships
The constitutional relationship applied to students enrolled in public institutions is the one receiving primary focus in the recent literature on students in higher education. Before *Dixon*, this relationship was nonexistent in the eyes of the court. In fact, in a case decided not long before *Dixon*, the Second Circuit Court of Appeals affirmed the existence of in loco parentis and denied a student's due process and right to freedom of speech and press [*Steier* v. *New York State Education Commission*, 271 F.2d 150 (5th Cir. 1959)], ruling that attendance at a public institution was a privilege granted by the state and that the federal courts have no jurisdiction over the granting of those privileges.

Dixon v. *Alabama* reversed past precedent and brought the Constitution onto the campus, involving the denial of due process rights of black students dismissed from an Alabama public college for participation in a sit-in at a lunch counter at the state Capitol. The court ruled that the Fourteenth Amendment's due process and equal protection clauses define the student-institutional relationship at public institutions. As a result, the state must give students due process of law when either a liberty interest or property right is found to exist before denying a student access to the institution for the purpose of continuing his education. The Fourteenth Amendment thus becomes the vehicle requiring the state to guarantee those rights expressed and implied in the Bill of Rights to students enrolled in public institutions. The case also reflects a retreat from the courts' previous position of reluctance to adjudicate decisions about campus life (Kaplin 1979; Nordin 1982; Young 1976). And it reflects the position of higher education in society and the fact that higher education has become a primary source of upward mobility, fueling demands for accountability (Henry 1975).

Thus, a new and very specific relationship was born. Precedent-setting litigation in the 1960s and 1970s expanded and clarified the individual rights of students. Novel litigation in the late 1970s and 1980s has focused on the group rights of student organizations, particularly as they affect the First Amendment.

EVOLUTION OF CONSTITUTIONAL RIGHTS IN HIGHER EDUCATION

Public institutions fall under the obligations of a state to guarantee those rights enumerated in the First through Fourteenth Amendments. While private institutions are not under the same constitutional mandate as public institutions, constitutional protections are enforced at many private institutions on the basis of ethical—as opposed to legal—precedents. Litigation subsequent to *Dixon* shows the evolving case law, from the definition of individual rights in the 1960s and 1970s to the definition of First Amendment issues involving groups in the 1980s.

The Evolution of Individual Rights

Dixon v. *Alabama* was clearly a landmark decision. The case involved a group of black students who had participated in civil rights protests in Montgomery and were notified by letter of their dismissal from Alabama State College. The students sued, demanding proper notification of the charges and a hearing before dismissal from a public institution and alleging rights guaranteed by the due process clause of the Fourteenth Amendment. The students alleged that the act of enrollment at a public institution did not result in the relinquishment of constitutional rights. The Fifth Circuit Court held that ". . . the state cannot condition the granting of even a privilege upon the renunciation of the constitutional rights to procedural due process" (p. 156) and noted that education was both "essential and vital" to productive citizenship in a modern society. The result was that the court not only had brought the Constitution to bear on public institutions in their various relationships but also had buried past reluctance to intervene in educational matters previously left to the college. This case opened the doors to the campus, facilitating the litigation of other challenges in education outside the constitutional realm (Millington 1979, p. 5).

The importance of *Dixon* is emphasized not only in the long line of case law that followed but also in the literature, which labels the case as "still very instructive" in describing due process requirements in disciplinary dismissal cases involving students (Kaplin 1985, p. 303). The *Dixon* court stated:

The notice should contain a statement of the specific charges and grounds [that], if proven, would justify expulsion under regulations of the board of education. The nature of the hearing should vary depending upon the circumstances of the particular case. The case before us requires something more than an informal interview with an administrative authority of the college. By its nature, a charge of misconduct, as opposed to a failure to meet the scholastic standards of the college, depends upon a collection of the facts concerning the charged misconduct, easily colored by the point of view of the witnesses. In such circumstances, a hearing [that] gives the board or the administrative authorities of the college an opportunity to hear both sides in considerable detail is best suited to protect the rights of all involved. This is not to imply that a full-dress judicial hearing, with the right to cross-examine witnesses, is required. Such a hearing, with the attending publicity and disturbance of college activities, might be detrimental to the college's educational atmosphere and impractical to carry out. Nevertheless, the rudiments of an adversary proceeding may be preserved without encroaching upon the interests of the college [emphasis added]. *In the instant case, the student should be given the names of the witnesses against him and an oral or written report on the facts to which each witness testifies. He should also be given the opportunity to present to the board, or at least to an administrative official of the college, his own defense against the charges and to produce either oral testimony or written affidavits of witnesses in his behalf. If the hearing is not before the board directly, the results and findings of the hearing should be presented in a report open to the student's inspection. If these rudimentary elements of fair play are followed in a case of misconduct of this particular type, we feel that the requirements of due process of law will have been fulfilled* (pp. 158–59).

While *Dixon* is still instructive about requirements for due process, other cases further clarify not only this right but other constitutional rights that states must guarantee to students at public institutions. By the beginning of the 1970s, many of these individual rights had been clearly defined.

Due Process

While *Dixon* defined the requirements of a notice and a hearing, other cases would further refine those requirements. The most frequently cited case providing a very detailed description of requirements for due process was *Esteban* v. *Central Missouri State College* [277 F. Supp. 649 (W.D. Mo. 1967)] (see Kaplin 1985, p. 304; Kemerer and Deutsch 1979, p. 351). In *Esteban,* the court listed a number of requirements to ensure due process: (1) written notification of the specific charges 10 days before the hearing; (2) a hearing before the agent(s) empowered to expel; (3) an opportunity to inspect documents or items the institution will present at the hearing; (4) the opportunity for the accused to present his own stories and witnesses on his behalf; (5) a determination of outcome based solely on the evidence presented at the hearing; (6) a written statement of the hearing agent's findings; and (7) the right of the accused, at his expense, to record the hearing (Kaplin 1985, p. 304).

The specificity of these requirements may have resulted from the facts of that case, limiting somewhat their application to all due process cases (Kemerer and Deutsch 1979, p. 351). More recent cases seem to indicate less rigidity than the due process proscriptions in *Esteban. Henson* v. *Honor Committee of the University of Virginia* [719 F.2d 69 (4th Cir. 1983)], for example, supports the notion of administrative flexibility in meeting requirements for due process (Kaplin 1985, p. 304).

Other cases have reviewed other specific requirements concerning due process. *Wright* v. *Texas Southern University* [392 F.2d 728 (5th Cir. 1968)], for example, indicates that an institution need make only a "best effort" to deliver a written notice to a student, and *Jenkins* v. *Louisiana State Board of Education* [506 F.2d 992 (5th Cir. 1975)] describes the contents of the notice as adequately defining the charges, while allowing for additional charges to be developed as a result of factual information evolving from the hearing. *Gross* v. *Lopez* [419 U.S. 565 (1975)], a case involving secondary education that is applicable to higher education, ruled that suspensions before a hearing could take place only when it was determined that continued attendance of the accused "poses a continuing danger to persons or property or an ongoing threat of disrupting the academic process." A subsequent hearing must take place as soon as possible (p. 583).

The right to counsel was also clarified. While the right to counsel is not an absolute right, it is clear that, if the institution uses legal counsel, the student must also be allowed access to counsel [*Barker* v. *Hardway,* 283 F. Supp. 228 (S.D. W.Va. 1968); *French* v. *Bashful,* 303 F. Supp. 1333 (E.D. La. 1969); Young 1976, p. 13].

These cases demonstrate the evolution of the courts' definition of what constitutes due process. More recent cases, such as *Henson,* indicate the courts' willingness to provide some flexibility in meeting the requirements of due process. While this flexibility is reflected in the case law, some of the literature does not reflect the same level of flexibility in the application of requirements for due process. Some authors promote rigidity and complexity in meeting requirements for due process that may go beyond the courts' intentions but serve desires for conservative risk management. One argument, for example, advocates the establishment of a standard of proof in disciplinary cases called "the clear and convincing arguments standard" (labeled as the middle ground and used in equity cases), which lies between "the reasonable doubt standard" (used in criminal prosecutions) and "the preponderance of evidence standard" (used in civil cases) (Long 1985). While lawyers might feel comfortable with these definitions, laymen find them very confusing, with the result that judicial proceedings take on the tenor of strict judicial proscriptions. Disciplinary hearings conducted under strict judicial proscriptions are outside the intent of *Dixon* and are not consistent with recent litigation and an institution's educational objectives. It is strict legal proscriptions that have resulted in student affairs administrators calling for disciplinary procedures that lend themselves to developmental objectives for students while protecting the rudiments of fundamental fairness and due process spelled out in *Dixon* and subsequent case law (Ostroth and Hill 1978). By following the court's directions in *Esteban,* one could walk the tightrope between concerns about students' development and sound risk management.

Due Process in Academic Dismissal
Courts have traditionally deferred to academicians in academic decisions (Hendrickson and Lee 1983; Kaplin 1985,

p. 307), and cases involving faculty employment and academic dismissal reinforce the concept of deference (Hendrickson and Lee 1983; Hobbs 1981). Academic deference forms the locus for the case law involving academic dismissal.

The controlling case in the area of academic dismissal is *Board of Curators of the University of Missouri* v. *Horowitz* [435 U.S. 78 (1978)], which considered a medical student dismissed for failing on several occasions to meet the clinical requirements for graduation from medical school. Dismissal was the final result of several years of oral and written notification of deficiencies and opportunities for reevaluation by different professionals. The court stated:

Academic
deference
forms the
locus for the
case law
involving
academic
dismissal.

> *Academic evaluation of a student, in contrast to disciplinary determinations, bears little resemblance to the judicial and administrative fact-finding proceedings to which we have traditionally attached a full-hearing requirement. . . . The decision to dismiss respondent, by comparison, rested on the academic judgment of school officials that she did not have the necessary clinical ability to perform adequately as a medical doctor and was making insufficient progress toward that goal. Such a judgment is by its nature more subjective and evaluative than the typical factual questions presented in the average disciplinary decision. Like the decision of an individual professor as to the proper grade for a student in his course, the determination whether to dismiss a student for academic reasons requires an expert evaluation of cumulative information and is not readily adapted to the procedural tools of judicial or administrative decision-making* (pp. 90–91).

Future litigation in the area of academic dismissal will find past precedent yielding opinions "heavily weighted in favor of the academic community" *(Willamette Law Journal* 1979, p. 590). *Regents of the University of Michigan* v. *Ewing* [106 S.Ct. 507 (1985)] gives additional strength to academic deference in academic decisions, although more recent decisions have distinguished plagiarism and cheating as disciplinary problems requiring due process [see *Crook* v. *Baker,* 584 F. Supp. 1531 (E.D. Mich. 1984); *Tully* v. *Orr,* 608 F. Supp. 1222 (E.D. N.Y. 1985)]. The rationale for these holdings is that charges of cheating or plagiarism implicate a liberty interest (harm to one's good name) necessitating due process. The assignment of grades and the determination of academic performance continue for the time being, absent a showing of arbitrary and capricious action, to be nonjusticiable issues.

Rights to Privacy

The Supreme Court has enumerated various rights to privacy as emanating from several amendments in the Bill of Rights. The benchmark case enumerating these rights is *Griswold* v. *Connecticut* [381 U.S. 479 (1965)]. Justice Douglas, delivering the majority opinion of the court and citing the First, Third, Fourth, and Fifth Amendments, noted that "specific guarantees in the Bill of Rights have penumbras, formed by emanations that help give them life and substance" (p. 481). These amendments create a zone of privacy guaranteed to all citizens. The interpretation of the existence of this zone of privacy came to higher education in the form of questions of search and seizure in institutionally operated residence halls. Students do not abdicate basic rights to privacy because they are living in the institution's residence halls (Young 1976, p. 18). *Moore* v. *Student Affairs Committee of Troy State University* [284 F. Supp. 725 (M.D. Ala. 1968)] established the institution's right to enter and search a student's room when it has reason to believe that the student is using the room either for illegal activity or in a way that threatens the educational atmosphere fostered at the institution. *Piazzola* v. *Watkins* [442 F. Supp. 284 (5th Cir. 1971)] noted the institution's right to inspect the premises and to enter in times of emergency but ruled that such authority to maintain discipline and an educational atmosphere may not be transferred to civil authorities. *Speakes* v. *Grantham* [317 F. Supp. 1253 (S.D. Miss. 1970)] found that evidence found in plain view during the *legal entrance* of a student's room is admissible in court.

The case law in this area indicates that the level of privacy established by the courts is less than that guaranteed to a citizen in the community. Students are protected from warrantless searches by law enforcement officers but must allow institutional authorities access to their rooms for purposes of inspection and when the "educational atmosphere" of the residence hall is seriously threatened. It would behoove administrators to read the literature carefully and to discuss these matters with legal counsel before developing or implementing policies that may violate students' rights to privacy (see Edwards and Nordin 1979, 1983; Kaplin 1985; Kemerer and Deutsch 1979; Young 1976).

The Expansion of Individual Rights by Federal Regulation
If the 1960s is characterized as "the decade of the ascent of individual rights," then the 1970s should be characterized as "the decade of federal regulation" (Hobbs 1978). Federal regulation has given rise to "the new torts" under the rubric of legal liability (Hendrickson and Mangum 1977). Litigation in the 1970s surrounding Title IX of the Education Amendments of 1972, for example, significantly affected institutional admission practices and athletics (Hendrickson and Mangum 1977, pp. 32–33).

More recent litigation has narrowed the scope of Title IX by addressing the issue of whether Title IX covers employment (Hendrickson and Lee 1983). *Grove City College* v. *Bell* [104 S.Ct. 1211 (1984)] and *North Haven* v. *Bell* [456 U.S. 509 (1982)] defined a program covered under the act as one receiving direct federal financial assistance and held that federal student aid money can be traced only to the specific program receiving that aid (for example, the financial aid office). These cases essentially narrowed the scope of Title IX so as to render it almost impotent; however, the litigation of the 1980s has thus far not diminished the changes this legislation brought about in the areas of admission and recruitment in academic programs and in the enhancement and in some cases creation of women's athletic programs.

The Buckley Amendment [the Family Educational Rights and Privacy Act of 1974 (41 CFR 9062)] defined requirements for students' and parents' access to their own records under threat of loss of federal funding for noncompliance. While little litigation has occurred in this area, it did have a significant effect on the way institutions keep records and give students access to those records.

The Rehabilitation Act of 1973 (29 U.S.C. 701) set guidelines prohibiting discrimination in the admission and hiring of "otherwise qualified handicapped individuals" in programs receiving federal financial assistance. In the area of admissions, the Court in *Southeastern Community College* v. *Davis* [442 U.S. 397 (1979)] set the valid criteria that can be used in determining the admissibility of an "otherwise qualified handicapped individual," noting that criteria used in the performance of essential job functions need not be modified to accommodate the handicapped individual; such individuals should instead be evaluated as able to perform those criteria despite the handicap.

Federal regulations and subsequent litigation had sweeping effects on higher education in the area of employment during the 1970s through legislation and enforcement of Titles VI and VII. Affecting both students and employees in their relations with institutions, these regulations give credence to the characterization of the 1970s as the decade of federal regulation. The seventies not only saw the clarification of the courts' reluctance to become involved in academic matters but also was a time when the First Amendment would have a significant effect on the recognition of student groups. And the refinement of the issues involving the First Amendment would continue into the 1980s.

First Amendment Rights

A number of First Amendment rights involving freedom of speech—the freedoms of press, speech, assembly, and association—evolved in public institutions.

Tinker v. *Des Moines Independent Community School District* [393 U.S. 503 (1969)] established the existence of First Amendment rights in educational settings. The case involved the prohibition of the wearing of armbands in protest against the Vietnam War. The Court ruled that the wearing of armbands was pure speech, in no way disrupting the educational processes of the high school, and thus established that nondisruptive speech is a protected right at a public educational institution.

Healy v. *James* [408 U.S. 169 (1972)] applied protections of the First Amendment to college students equal to those applied to citizens of the local community; the Court stated that colleges are the "marketplace of ideas" where "academic freedom" should be protected (p. 180). In *Buttney* v. *Smiley* [281 F. Supp. 280 (D. Colo. 1968)], however, the court found that activity preventing others from speaking or participating in institutional business is not protected by the First Amendment. At the same time, speakers cannot be denied access to the institutional forum where speech is permitted unless there is reason to know that the words uttered will result in disruptive activity by the speakers or onlookers or create imminent danger to the safety of the speaker or onlookers [see *Stacy* v. *Williams, 306 F. Supp. 963* (N.D. Miss. 1969)]. Rules may be set governing "time, place, and manner" of the speech, but such rules should not be used to inhibit speech [see *Bayless* v. *Maritime, 430 F.2d 873* (5th Cir. 1970)]. Regulations that go to the content of speech are suspect and as a general rule will not be upheld in court except in the event of disruption or imminent danger *[Papish* v. *Board of Curators of the University of Missouri, 410 U.S. 667* (1972)].

Healy and other cases are examples of the use of a prior restraint on speech or the content of school newspapers, and *Hammond* v. *South Carolina State College* [272 F. Supp. 947 (D. S.C. 1967)] is a classic example of a prior restraint (Kaplin 1985, p. 319). In that case, a student was expelled from campus for holding a demonstration without the president's prior approval. As is true historically of prior restraint, the court held it to be in violation of the student's First Amendment rights.

The most frequently cited case involving the editorial content of a school newspaper is *Dickey* v. *Alabama* [273 F. Supp. 613 (M.D. Ala. 1967)], where a student editor was suspended for an editorial that was critical of the governor. The court found that, while the school was not obligated to provide financial support to the student newspaper, the editor's freedom of speech would be violated if he were suspended for the editorial content of the paper.

In the absence of a showing of material disruption, interference with the rights of others, or that the publication is obscene, censorship and control of such publications by college officials is deemed an unwarranted interference with protected constitutional rights [Young 1976, p. 5, citing *Joyner* v. *Whiting*, 477 F.2d 456 (4th Cir. 1973)].

Antonelli v. *Hammond* [308 F. Supp. 1329 (D. Mass. 1970)] noted that obscenity can be restrained, but the courts have set very narrow guidelines that place the burden of proving obscenity squarely on the shoulders of the institution (see Kaplin 1985, p. 335).

A key case involving rights of association was *Healy* v. *James,* which considered the denial of an institution's official recognition of Students for a Democratic Society (SDS).

The mere disagreement of the President with the group's philosophy affords no reason to deny it recognition. As repugnant as these views may have been, especially to one with President James' responsibility, the mere expression of them would not justify the denial of First Amendment rights. Whether petitioners did in fact advocate a philosophy of "destruction" thus becomes immaterial. The College, acting here as the instrumentality of the State, may not restrict speech or association simply because it finds the views expressed by any group to be abhorrent (p. 175).

The principles established in *Healy* were followed in a number of cases involving organizations advocating homosexual rights [see *Gay Students Organization of the University of New Hampshire* v. *Bonner,* 367 F. Supp. 1088 (D. N.H. 1974); *aff'd,* 509 F.2d 652 (1st Cir. 1974); *Gay Liberation* v. *University of Missouri,* 558 F.2d 848 (8th Cir. 1977)]. These cases held that failure to recognize such organizations violated a student's rights of association and that recognition could not be withheld based on the group's lawful advocacies.

First Amendment issues continued to evolve in the eighties. The next three sections outline the primary litigation of the decade: rights of association as they affect recognition of groups and their use of facilities; rights of association as they affect the collection and allocation of mandatory student activity fees; and the right, under commercial speech controlling regulatory schemes, to limit solicitation on campus.

RECOGNITION OF STUDENT ORGANIZATIONS AND USE OF CAMPUS FACILITIES: First Amendment Boundaries

This chapter reviews several rights of association and their effect on the recognition of religious and gay organizations and on regulations governing use of facilities.

Distinctions between Public and Private Colleges

The actions of public colleges and universities are considered state actions, and, because they are considered agents of government, the institutions are bound to comply with the First and Fourteenth Amendments. Private colleges and universities, however, are neither agencies of the state nor an arm of state government. As suggested in the last section, numerous legal rulings have held that private institutions, unlike their public counterparts, are not legally bound by constitutional standards for the protection of private persons and institutions unless strong indications exist of state control.

The major distinction between private and public colleges is that public colleges have both contractual and constitutional relationships, while private colleges have only contractual relationships with their students (Hollander, Young, and Gehring 1985).

Recognition of Organizations

According to the First Amendment, "Congress shall make no law . . . abridging the freedom of speech, or of the press; or the right of the people peaceably to assemble," and students have not hesitated during the past decade to sue college and university administrators who limit or deny their First Amendment right of association or recognition. The U.S. Supreme Court ruled in *Healy* v. *James* [408 U.S. 169 (1972)] that the First Amendment right of freedom of association applied to students and, as a corollary, that official recognition from the college or university was necessary to implement that right.

In *Healy,* students at Central Connecticut State College attempted to organize a local chapter of Students for a Democratic Society. Following procedures established by the college, the students filed the request for official recognition as a campus organization with the Student Affairs Committee. The committee, while satisfied that the statement of purpose was clear and unobjectionable on its face, was concerned over the relationship between the local group and the national SDS organization. In response to inquiries, representatives of the proposed organization said they would not affiliate with any national group and that their group would remain "completely independent" *(Healy 1972, p. 172)*. The committee ultimately approved the application and recommended to the president of the college that the organization be granted official recognition.

The president rejected the committee's recommendation, asserting that the organization's philosophy was at odds with the college's commitment to academic freedom and that the organization would be a disruptive influence on campus. The Supreme Court rejected the president's argument:

> *While the freedom of association is not explicitly set out in the [First] Amendment, it has long been held to be implicit in the freedoms of speech, assembly, and petition. There can be no doubt that denial of official recognition, without justification, to college organizations burdens or abridges that associational right* (p. 169).

Healy thus makes it clear that a state college or university may not restrict speech or association simply because it finds the views expressed by a group abhorrent (p. 170).

Denial of Benefits of Recognition
To understand the severity of the burden placed on rights of association by denial of recognition, one must be aware of the meaning of such recognition. Courts have generally accepted official recognition of groups to mean that the college or university "acknowledges and sanctions the existence of" the group, not that it necessarily "approves" any religious, political, economic, or philosophical position of the organization. Official recognition usually conveys various benefits and privileges made available by college officials only to recognized student groups. These benefits may include but are not limited to:

1. *The privilege of scheduling campus facilities for meetings and activities, usually rent free;*
2. *The opportunity to lease a campus post office box;*
3. *The right to request funds from the student activities fund;*
4. *The privilege of using the school's name as part of the organization's name;*

5. *The opportunity to use school media;*
6. *The right to post notices and appropriate signs announcing activities;*
7. *The privilege of being listed in the student handbook and yearbook; and*
8. *The opportunity to qualify for awards and honors given to college student organizations* (Gibbs 1984, p. 38).

In the case of the college president's denial of official recognition in *Healy,* the Court found that the organization's ability to participate in the intellectual give and take of campus debate and to pursue its stated lawful purposes was limited by denial of access to the customary media for communicating with the administration, faculty members, and other students, concluding, "Such impediments cannot be viewed as insubstantial" *(Healy* 1972, p. 181).

Mere Advocacy versus Unlawful Action
While the Court allowed recognition of the SDS, it also—and equally as important—addressed the issue of justifiable nonrecognition. It concluded that an association's activities need not be tolerated if "they infringe reasonable campus rules, interrupt classes, or substantially interfere with the opportunity of other students to obtain an education" *(Healy* 1972, p. 189). This legal position was defined in more specific terms two years later in *Gay Students Organization of the University of New Hampshire* v. *Bonner* [367 F. Supp. 1088 (D. N.H. 1974); *aff'd,* 509 F.2d 652 (1st Cir. 1974)]:

> *The university may deny or withdraw all recognition of rights and privileges flowing there, from a student organization where there is a failure or refusal to abide by reasonable housekeeping rules or there is a demonstrated danger of violence or disruption of the university's educational mission or there has been a violation of criminal law by organization or by its members at a function sponsored by organization* (p. 1088).

The courts do not require colleges and universities to recognize organizations, but once institutions elect to sanction some groups, legal precedent indicates that courts will

. . . A state college or university may not restrict speech or association simply because it finds the views expressed by a group abhorrent.

mandate the recognition of all student groups, providing three criteria have been met. First, the group must have complied with all procedural requirements and must agree to abide by regulations governing time, place, and manner of speech. Second, the group must not demonstrate a danger of violence or disruption to the institution's educational purpose. Third, neither the organization nor its members may violate the criminal law during or through a group function (Gibbs 1979, p. 486).

The Public Forum Doctrine on Campus

The public forum doctrine has emerged from the Supreme Court's rulings involving the First Amendment rights of free speech and association and the equal protection clause of the Fourteenth Amendment. Broadly defined, a public forum "is a medium enabling people, individually or collectively, to exercise their speech, association, or petition rights for the advancement of public beliefs" (Bauer 1983, p. 136). The basic concept of the public forum doctrine is that freedom of speech guarantees speakers the right to use public places for expression as well as association. In practice, the First Amendment guarantees a right for citizens to use public forums for effectively exercising their rights, particularly in places traditionally used for speeches and association, such as streets and parks. Such rights are subject to reasonable regulations governing time, place, and manner if ample alternate channels of communication are left open [*Perry Education Association* v. *Perry Local Educators Association,* 460 U.S. 37 (1983)].

Issues of primary interest and concern to college administrators are what constitutes a public forum and what are reasonable restrictions on time, place, and manner. Courts have been consistent in viewing college campuses as places for thought, a forum for the free exchange of ideas. The student union building, for example, is a public forum, open to all student groups [*Chess* v. *Widmar,* 635 F.2d 1310 (8th Cir. 1980); *aff'd, Widmar* v. *Vincent,* 454 U.S. 263 (1981)].

The Supreme Court clearly described the public forum doctrine in *Police Department* v. *Mosley* [408 U.S. 92 (1972)]:

> *The First Amendment means that government may not grant the use of a forum to people whose views it finds*

acceptable, but deny use to those wishing to express less favored or more controversial views. And it may not select which issues are worth discussing or debating in public facilities. There is an "equality of status in the field of ideas," and government must afford all points of view an equal opportunity to be heard. Once a forum is opened up to assembly or speaking by some groups, government may not prohibit others from assembling or speaking on the basis of what they intend to say. Selective exclusions from a public forum may not be based on content alone, and may not be justified by reference to content alone (p. 96).

In *Grayned* v. *City of Rockford* [408 U.S. 104 (1972)], the Supreme Court addressed *reasonable* regulations governing time, place, and manner, asserting that "[t]he nature of a place [and] the pattern of its normal activities" dictate what constitutes "reasonable" (p.116).

While locations like streets, sidewalks, and parks traditionally have been held to be public forums because of their historical association with the broadest scope of First Amendment activities, other public facilities have achieved the special status of public forums as a result of their designation by authorities as a place for exchange of views among members of the public *(Perry Education Association* v. *Perry Local Educators Association* 1983). Finally, public facilities that have been created for purposes closely linked to expression although not for unrestricted public interchange of ideas have been recognized as "semipublic forums" (Howarth and Connell 1981, p. 115).

In summary, the consensus of the courts appears to be that public college campuses fall at least within the category of "semipublic" and thus are subject to the principle that only non-content-based, reasonable restrictions of time, place, and manner may be placed on expression therein *(Chess* v. *Widmar* 1980; *aff'd, Widmar* v. *Vincent* 1981).

Religious Organizations at Public Colleges

The primary issue involving religious organizations at public colleges is whether a state college or university, which makes its facilities available for the activities of recognized student organizations, may close its facilities to a group desiring to use the "public" facilities for religious discussion and/or worship. The Supreme Court addressed this question in *Widmar* v. *Vincent* [454 U.S. 263 (1981)].

The *Widmar* litigation began when Cornerstone, a recognized student religious group at the University of Missouri at Kansas City, was denied continued access to university facilities. The university had actively encouraged student organizations, had officially recognized more than 100 such groups, and had regularly provided facilities for recognized groups. Cornerstone regularly applied for university space in which to conduct its meetings and received permission to use the facilities between 1973 and 1977. In 1977, however, the university decided to enforce a 1972 ruling by the Board of Trustees that prohibited the use of university buildings or grounds "for purposes of religious worship or religious teaching" *(Widmar* 1981, p. 272).

The students sued the university, alleging that because religious worship is constitutionally protected speech, UMKC's regulations restricting access to campus facilities violated their First Amendment rights of free speech and religion. The university countered that the discriminatory language in the challenged regulation was necessary to prevent state support of religion in violation of the establishment clause. The federal district court upheld the university, concluding that its restrictive regulation was indeed appropriate to prevent a breach of the Establishment of Religion Clause of the First Amendment *[Chess* v. *Widmar,* 480 F. Supp. 907 (W.D. Mo. 1979); *rev'd,* 635 F.2d 1310 (8th Cir. 1980)]. The Court of Appeals reversed the lower court, finding that UMKC's policy was an unconstitutional attempt to regulate the content of speech without showing a compelling justification.

The Supreme Court upheld the Court of Appeals:

Having created a forum generally open to student groups, a state university may not practice content-based exclusion of religious speech when that exclusion is not narrowly drawn to achieve a state interest in the separation of church and state (Widmar v. *Vincent* 1981, p. 264).

Thus, the Court directed college and university administrators to treat religious speech as secular speech in their recognition of student organizations and their policies regarding the use of institutional facilities.

The Establishment Clause

The Supreme Court since 1947 has interpreted the establishment clause to require that government must not only avoid giving preference to one religion over another but also must refrain from directly affecting any religious activities [*Everson* v. *Board of Education*, 330 U.S. 1 (1947)]. It has not, however, described so definitively the scope of the boundaries of the establishment clause, vacillating between a strict interpretation of the clause requiring total separation of church and state and a more liberal definition allowing varying degrees of interplay between the two [*Zorach* v. *Clauson*, 343 U.S. 306 (1952)].

In *Widmar*, the university argued that its need to comply with the establishment clause was a compelling reason and it was therefore justified in prohibiting Cornerstone from using the university's facilities. This position provided a different and somewhat unusual twist for the Supreme Court, in that the case had characteristics of the establishment, free exercise, and freedom of speech clauses.

The Court acknowledged that UMKC's interest in complying with the establishment clause could be termed "compelling" but that a policy of equal access would not violate the establishment clause. The Court concluded no justification existed for the university's content-based discrimination because a nondiscriminatory alternative was available (*Widmar* v. *Vincent* 1981). It apparently reasoned that when the two clauses collide head on, as they did in this case, the establishment clause must bow to the interests protected by the free exercise clause. Thus, the Court's ruling was based on First Amendment guarantees. Colleges and universities may not discriminate against student religious organizations and their access to university space on the basis of content, absent showing a compelling state interest. To do so would be to violate students' rights of free speech and association under the First Amendment.

Gay Student Organizations

Gay student organizations are often the most visible and active groups on college campuses today; perhaps in no other area in recent years have the asserted First Amend-

ment rights of students clashed so with the will of college administrators (Stanley 1983–84, p. 398). One of the most recent rulings involving the recognition of gay student organizations on the public college campus is *Gay Student Services* v. *Texas A&M University* [737 F.2d 1317 (5th Cir. 1984)], in which the U.S. Court of Appeals reversed the district court's decision upholding the state university's refusal to officially recognize the homosexual student group. The Court of Appeals's ruling held that the asserted justifications for the university's refusal to recognize the group were insufficient to justify the infringement of the group's First Amendment rights (p. 1318).

Administrators at Texas A&M registered an appeal with the Supreme Court, but in April 1985 the Court denied rehearing and dismissed the appeal, stating:

> *The state-supported university's refusal to recognize gay student organization violated the First Amendment; the district court's finding of fact that gay student organization was fraternal or social organization of type generally not recognized by university and that state had interest in preventing certain results that would flow from recognition were clearly erroneous* [105 S.Ct. 1860 (1985)].

In *Student Coalition for Gay Rights* v. *Austin Peay State University* [477 F. Supp. 1267 (M.D. Tenn. 1979)], administrators at the university presented several reasons to the court for not recognizing a gay student organization: (1) recognition would give credibility to homosexual behavior and tend to expand violations of state law prohibiting homosexual behavior; (2) recognition might lead to increased personal and psychological stress for people troubled about their sexual identity; (3) recognition would not be consistent with the university's educational goals; and (4) administrators were concerned about how the community outside the university would react if the coalition were recognized (p. 1269).

The district court rejected all four arguments, noting that by its failure to recognize the student group, "the University created a significant abridgment of their First Amendment rights" (p. 1272).

Two years later, the Board of Regents of the University of Oklahoma refused to recognize the Gay Activists Alliance (GAA), using as its justifications that: (1) it had a duty to ensure that the purposes of recognized groups reflected prevailing standards in the community; (2) behavior endorsed by GAA violated state law; (3) the university had a duty to protect the health, welfare, morals, and education of students; (4) recognition of the group would constitute endorsement; and (5) members of GAA suffered no infringement of constitutional rights by the university's not recognizing it [*Gay Activists Alliance* v. *Board of Regents of University of Oklahoma*, 638 P.2d 1116 (Okla. 1981)].

The Oklahoma Supreme Court ruled that the regents had not met their burden of proof relative to their justifications and that GAA was entitled to recognition as a university organization. When the denial of recognition is based on mere suspicion, unpopularity, and fear of what might occur and is achieved by state action that burdens rights of association, resulting in the lessening of an organization's ability to effectuate legal purposes, guaranteed freedoms have been violated (p. 1122).

The courts emphasized, however, that recognition by the university did not preclude *regulation* by the university. Drawing once again from the *Healy* standard, the courts ruled that reasonable regulations as to time, place, and manner of activity that are not unduly burdensome may be imposed equally upon all university student organizations.

Wood v. *Davison* [351 F. Supp. 543 (N.D. Ga. 1972)] involved the University of Georgia's denial of school facilities for a conference and dance by a student group called the Committee on Gay Education. The district court found that university officials had violated the students' First Amendment rights of assembly and association by denying them use of facilities open to all recognized campus organizations. After discussing the merits of the case, the court established three possible grounds upon which denial of use of campus facilities might be based: (1) the group's refusal to abide by reasonable college regulations; (2) demonstrated danger of violence or disruption at the meeting; and (3) a potential violation of state or federal law by the meeting itself. (For example, a meeting that contemplated criminal activity would be a basis for denial.)

Each of these grounds requires evidence to support an institution's denial of the organization's use. The court made explicit the university's responsibility following such a denial, however, requiring the university: (1) to give notice to the requesting organization within a reasonable time before the date planned for the activity, stating the grounds for denial; (2) to provide the organization an opportunity to eliminate the bases of denial if the irregularity can be cured; and (3) to give the organization an opportunity to respond to the grounds for denial, that is, some reasonable opportunity for the organization to meet the university's contentions. No requirement exists that this procedure consists of a "full-blown" adversary proceeding. The court noted that, should a basis of denial arise after approval, the university need not sit idly by and wait but may take steps to curtail violence, disruption, criminal activity, or conduct proscribed by applicable university rules and regulations *(Wood* v. *Davison* 1972, pp. 555–57).

In summary, the *Wood* court succinctly stated the dilemma of administrators, at least in the public sector, vis-à-vis their treatment of homosexual groups:

University presidents have the unenviable position of trying to maintain a precarious balance between the rights of members of the academic community and the wishes of the taxpayers and alumni who support that community. Nevertheless, it is not the prerogative of college officials to impose their own preconceived notions and ideals on the campus by choosing among proposed organizations, providing access to some and denying a forum to those with which they do not agree (p. 549).

Gay Student Organizations at Private Colleges
In the continuation of a six-year-old gay rights case, a three-judge panel of the District of Columbia's Court of Appeals reversed a trial court's ruling and ordered Georgetown University to grant official recognition to two organizations for homosexual students *[Gay Rights Coalition* v. *Georgetown University,* 496 A.2d 567 (D.C. Cir. 1985)]. Citing the Supreme Court's 1983 mandate in *Bob Jones University* v. *United States* [461 U.S. 574 (1983)], the D.C. court ruled that the District's 1977 Human Rights Act

established an "overriding governmental interest" in ending discrimination against homosexuals that is a sufficiently strong public policy to justify some infringement on the Jesuit university's religious freedom. (In the *Bob Jones* ruling, the university lost its federal tax exemption because a ban on interracial dating was found to violate federal laws aimed at preventing racial discrimination, which was viewed as a significant national public policy.)

The full District of Columbia Court of Appeals vacated the *Georgetown University* decision and docketed the case for review *[Gay Rights Coalition* v. *Georgetown University* [496 A.2d 587 (D.C. Cir. 1985)]. Lawyers representing both Georgetown University and the two student groups presented competing arguments to the D.C. Court of Appeals in October 1985 *(Chronicle of Higher Education* 23 October 1985), but as of publication of this monograph, the Court of Appeals had not handed down its decision. Whatever and whenever the ruling is determined, both sides indicate that the case will eventually be appealed to the Supreme Court.

Summary

Healy established that rights of association identified as part of the First Amendment apply to institutions and policies regulating student organizations. Institutions cannot deny or restrict speech or association simply because they find an organization's views abhorrent. The rationale for this position is partly the result of the courts' view that official recognition is nothing more than acknowledgment of the existence of the group and does not connote approval of the ideas or positions espoused by the group. Benefits accrued by recognition allow the group to participate in the intellectual give and take of an institution whose espoused purpose is to promote academic freedom. Once an institution recognizes an organization, it must award recognition free from bias based on the political, religious, or philosophical views of the organization.

Recognition can be withheld, however, from groups that are disruptive or violent or have committed a criminal offense. The burden of proof is on the institution to show than any of these rationales exist.

Denial of recognition to organizations that advocate the repeal of criminal statutes but do not commit criminal acts is not a constitutionally acceptable rationale. Cases involving gay organizations are examples; the courts have consistently upheld their right to recognition at public institutions. In private institutions, local statutes prohibiting discrimination based on sexual preference have been used to argue that a public policy would require private institutions to recognize gay organizations. This litigation, following the arguments in the *Bob Jones* case, is working its way through the court system.

Finally, two cases raised questions concerning institutional policies denying religious organizations access to facilities based on provisions for separation of church and state in state constitutions and the establishment clause of the First Amendment. The courts found that the equal access policy of allowing groups recognition and use of facilities regardless of positions advocated struck a delicate balance among the freedom of association, free exercise, and establishment clauses of the First Amendment.

COLLECTION AND ALLOCATION OF MANDATORY STUDENT ACTIVITY FEES

Assessing mandatory student activity fees to students has become common practice at colleges and universities. Though no legal challenge to the practice has yet reached the Supreme Court, lower court rulings have held that charging such mandatory fees is constitutional. The rulings from litigation involving such fees and those from analogous cases in noneducational areas have answered few important constitutional questions, however. Does the Constitution limit how the funds may be used? Does the use of these funds affect how a college or university may collect the fees? And conversely, can certain methods of collection run contrary to constitutional limits on the use of the funds?

As the frequency and variety of students' attacks on the nature of mandatory fees increase, the difficult task remains for college and university administrators to assimilate what guidance the courts have given and formulate legal and equitable policies concerning the collection and allocation of mandatory student activity fees.

The courts cite several parallel cases involving mandatory dues for trade unions when ruling on mandatory student activity fees. Teachers who were not members of a teachers union, for example, were required to pay a service charge equal to union dues [*Abood* v. *Detroit Board of Education,* 431 U.S. 209 (1977)], but the Supreme Court approved only that portion of the assessment "used to finance expenditures by the union for the purposes of collective bargaining, contract administration, and grievance adjustment" (p. 209). The union could not exact fees for political purposes from anyone who objected to its goals. The constitutional basis for this ruling is that a corollary of the First Amendment right to associate is the right not to associate. The fact that the appellants were compelled to make, rather than prohibited from making, contributions for political purposes works no less an infringement of their constitutional rights (p. 210).

The Seventh Circuit Court expanded the *Abood* ruling by scrutinizing not only the legal use of mandatory fees but the methods of their collection as well [*Perry* v. *Local Lodge 2569 of the International Association of Machinists and Aerospace Workers,* 708 F.2d 1258 (7th Cir. 1983)]. Even though a refund system allowed reimbursement to individual members who objected to certain uses of mandatory fees, the court held that such a union refund system

The constitutional basis for this ruling is that a corollary of the First Amendment right to associate is the right not to associate.

was inadequate to protect members' First Amendment rights not to be coerced into financing the union's political objectives.

While the *Abood* and *Perry* rulings make clear that First Amendment rights cannot be violated by the imposition of mandatory fees despite the method of their collection, these cases provide little information as to what analysis the courts employ when determining precisely when such a right has been violated. In *Lindenbaum* v. *City of Philadelphia* [584 F. Supp. 1190 (E.D. Pa. 1984)], where city employees claimed they were denied increases in pensions because they chose not to join a union, the district court explained the analysis used:

> *Government distinctions between persons similarly situated are constitutionally permissible if they are shown to be reasonably grounded in some legitimate government policy; those distinctions based on a "suspect classification" or substantially impinging upon "fundamental rights" cannot pass constitutional muster unless they satisfy substantially stricter scrutiny than mere rationality* (p. 1197).

The differential in the award of fringe benefits based on payment of union dues is a "suspect classification" that must be substantiated by a compelling governmental interest. The equal protection clause is the umbrella that places the differential treatment violating the First Amendment freedom of association clause under scrutiny; this test will be applied in other cases involving mandatory fees.

Allocation and Use of Mandatory Fees

Mandatory student activity fees are distributed to student groups and organizations in several ways. In 60 percent of schools surveyed in one recent study, student government associations have primary authority for appropriation, while in another 30 percent, an institutional official or body has the primary authority (Meaborn, Suddick, and Gibbs 1985). In those institutions where students have primary responsibility, internally established guidelines are often used for assistance, thus ensuring that institutional administrators assume at least an indirect role in the process. Courts have supported administrators' involvement by recognizing the university's power to intervene to the point of being able to prohibit or direct the use of certain funds allocated by the student government association [see *Maryland Public Interest Research Group* v. *Elkins,* 565 F.2d 864 (4th Cir. 1978); *cert. denied,* 435 U.S. 1008 (1978)].

The funds generated by mandatory student fees may be distributed on a prorated basis according to various student groups' requests, line items in the budget, assessment of need, or a formula for distribution. College administrators have broad power to intervene in the allocation of funds— to the extent of being able to insist that a student organization include a specific item in its budget. In *Associated Students, San Jose State University* v. *Trustees of California State Universities and Colleges* [128 Cal. Rptr. 601 (Cal. Ct. App. 1976)], for example, where the student government association omitted athletic grants-in-aid from its budget, the court ruled that "a state university or college president may reject a student body organization's budget or financial program when he reasonably concludes that it is not in conformity with the policy of the campus" (p. 601).

Despite the numerous methods used to allocate fees, these methods of appropriation have not themselves played a significant role in court challenges to the assessment of student fees. Litigation has focused almost exclusively on *use* of the fees, with the methods of their allocation having little or no bearing on the courts' ultimate rulings.

Religious objections

One category of challenges to student fees has alleged that certain uses of the mandatory fees violate students' First Amendment rights to freedom of religion. In *Erzinger* v. *Regents of the University of California* [187 Cal. Rptr. 164 (Cal. Ct. App. 1982)], for example, the objecting students charged that the university had infringed upon their First Amendment rights to free exercise of religion by exacting from them a fee used to pay for abortion counseling, abortion referral, and abortions. The California appellate court ruled that, to be exempt from paying that portion of the fee so used, the students had to "allege and prove the university coerced their religious beliefs or unreasonably interfered with their practice of religion" (p. 164). The students failed to provide such proof, as their payment of the fee neither prevented them from expressing their own views against abortion nor forced them to endorse abortions. In recognizing the regents' wide discretion over internal matters, the court held that it was not important that the primary focus of the program was the students' health and not their education, as "the Regents have the legal authority to assess mandatory student fees and utilize those fees for the benefit of its student population, even when those fees are not used directly to support the cost of specific education programs or services" (p. 164).

While not yet the subject of actual litigation, other expenditures of fees that elicit complaints based on religion include the purchase of alcohol for student social functions and payments to rock groups for campus performances. It is likely that the courts will use the reasoning of *Erzinger* and exercise minimal scrutiny over such use of fees, prohibiting them only when they coerce certain beliefs or interfere with personal religious choices and practices. Purchasing alcohol, for example, does not prevent students from abstaining from its consumption or expressing their views against its use.

Political objections

The other major category of challenges to use of mandatory student fees is politically oriented, with the offended students claiming violations of constitutionally protected freedoms to associate, speak, and express themselves. In this area too the courts have deferred to administrative discretion, but scrutiny of possible violations of constitutional rights is heightened compared to that applied to religious objections. Just as in the cases involving challenges to fees exacted in nonschool settings, the courts tend to engage in a constitutional balancing act, weighing the college's or university's interests in the use of the fees with students' First Amendment rights.

One of the earliest legal rulings to institute the balancing test was *Veed* v. *Schwartzkopf* [353 F. Supp. 149 (D. Neb. 1973); *aff'd mem.*, 478 F.2d 1407 (8th Cir. 1973); *cert. denied*, 414 U.S. 1135 (1974)], where mandatory student activity fees were used to fund the student newspaper, student government, and a guest speakers program. The complaining student argued that requiring him to pay a fee to subsidize programs that advanced views he found repugnant effectively forced him to become associated with those views, in violation of his First Amendment rights. The simple, clearcut rationale for the court's rejection of this argument was that the university had no direct control over the use of funds and thus was not advancing any particular view. The court also held that the university's educational program extended beyond the classroom, functioning to provide students with "a broad range of ideas in a variety of contexts" (p. 153).

The *Veed* court's ruling provided the foundation for the balancing test important in later decisions. While the court generally approved the university's right to impose mandatory fees, it made clear that such power is not unlimited. The institution's exacting and use of the monies cannot be arbitrary, cannot impose acceptance or practice of repugnant religious, political, or personal views, or cannot chill students' exercise of a constitutional right (p. 149).

The balancing test was the primary analytical tool used in *Good* v. *Associated Students, University of Washington* [542 P.2d 762 (Wash. 1975)], where the Supreme Court of Washington addressed the comparable funding of a student government association:

> *If we allow mandatory financial support to be unchecked, the plaintiff's rights may be meaningless. On the other hand, if we allow dissenters to withhold the minimal financial contributions required, we would permit a possible minority view to destroy or cripple a valuable learning adjunct of university life* (p. 768).

The court, depicting the university as an arena where conflicting ideas meet, ultimately approved the use of the mandatory fees when such use is lawful and "not the vehicle for the promotion of one particular viewpoint" (p. 763). A university can exact the fees even from students who oppose certain uses of the funds, regardless of their reasons. Those students cannot be compelled, however, to join an organization that "purports to represent *all* the students at the university" (p. 768).

While these rulings have generally provided the balancing test used in scrutinizing uses of mandatory fees for violations of constitutional rights, they do not show exactly how use of the fee is analyzed. These cases have merely set forth the test to be used and stated the result. They do not explain how the test is used nor why a constitutional right is violated in one situation and not in another, thus giving little guidance to college administrators facing immediate or prospective problems.

Methods of Collection
Student activity fees are collected through several different mechanisms. The most basic method is the standard, mandatory fee assessment, where each student must pay the activity fee along with tuition. No exceptions are made: The fees are simply a fact of student life. This form of collection is least protective of an individual's constitutional rights, but it is proper to the extent that it supports a broad forum of ideas, thus not promoting or hindering expression of any particular view. Because college and university officials have more control over the standard assessment, courts might tend to accord greater deference to the university's judgment that the funds support such a forum.

At the other extreme of methods of collection is the optional, check-off system, where the student must act affirmatively to initiate contributions to student groups, usually by checking a box on a form to indicate that he wishes the fee to be assessed. This system offers the greatest degree of protection to the student's constitutional rights, as he or she may choose which student groups to support.

Somewhere between these two extremes are the reverse check-off and refund systems, where the student must act affirmatively *not* to pay activity fees. Under the refund system, the fee is mandatory and automatically assessed, but the money is returned if—and only if—the student requests a refund. A refundable mandatory fee gives the dissenting student some protection, but it allows the group that the student opposes to use the money for a period of time and requires the individual to ask for the refund. The reverse check-off system is like the refund system in that it requires action not to pay, but it affords greater constitutional protection because the student has the chance to refuse the assessment at the outset, before the fees are ever charged to the student's account. Thus, by checking off the appropriate form, a student who finds a particular group or its policies distasteful may choose not to give that group even temporary use of the collected money. The reverse check-off system has met with approval in several courts, including the Sixth Circuit Court of Appeals [*Kentucky Educators Public Affairs Council* v. *Kentucky Registry of Election Finance*, 677 F.2d 1125 (6th Cir. 1982)].

One major question surrounding the various collection systems is whether, once a student raises a complaint about uses of certain fees, the method of collection will make a difference in the amount of scrutiny the courts use. *Stanley* v. *McGrath* [719 F.2d 279 (8th Cir. 1983)] is useful in trying to predict what the courts will ultimately decide on this question and on the more general issue of the constitutionality of the various collection schemes per se. In *Stanley,* public complaints over the contents of an issue of the school newspaper motivated university officials to change the method of the paper's funding from a mandatory fee exacted from all students to a refund system. The paper's editors brought suit, claiming the action adversely affected publication and violated their First Amendment rights. The Eighth Circuit reversed the district court's dismissal of the complaint, holding that the change in the method of funding had a chilling effect upon the newspaper and was thus unconstitutional. The court pointed to the fact that newspapers in other branches of the university did not suffer similar changes in funding, thus making the institution's actions purely punitive.

The *Stanley* ruling may be equally as important for what it does not say. The circuit court neither affirmed nor denied the district court's statement of the legal principle that it is constitutionally permissible for an institution to establish a fee refund system out of concern for the rights of opposing students not to fund views with which they disagree. Rather, it merely assumes "for present purposes that this is a constitutionally permissible motivation" (p. 283).

The *Stanley* court did not address the important question of how collection systems interact with use and allocation of fees.

In fact, students may have a First Amendment right not to be forced to buy a newspaper with which they disagree. Certainly a state could not pass a law requiring its residents to buy a particular newspaper, or any *newspaper, for that matter* (citing Abood). *On the other hand, the University may be within its rights in treating the* Daily *as a kind of bulletin board containing notices it wants students to see. It cannot make the students read a bulletin board, but it can buy one with compulsory student fees.* We express no view on these questions [emphasis added] (p. 283).

In refusing to express a view, the court does just that. It is clear, for instance, that the constitutional balancing test is still being used—and still being used without explanation as to how.

Thus, *Stanley* establishes that a refund system may not be used as a subterfuge to aid an institution in avoiding its constitutional responsibilities (Morton 1985). This holding, in conjunction with the previous quotation, implies that it is questionable at best that a refund system attached to an otherwise impermissible fee will make it suddenly permissible. Though the court does not express an opinion on this issue, it can be inferred that the collection scheme used really does not matter. If the fee and/or its use is itself judged unconstitutional through the balancing test, changing the method of collection will not make a difference.

The Galda Saga: The Latest View
The most recent and widely publicized legal ruling on the subject of mandatory student fees is the second Third Circuit appeal of *Galda* v. *Rutgers* [589 F. Supp. 479 (D. N.J. 1984); *rev'd* and *remanded,* 722 F.2d 1060 (3rd Cir. 1985)]. [See also *Galda* v. *Bloustein,* 686 F.2d 159 (3rd Cir. 1982).] Several Rutgers students claimed that a mandatory fee the university had imposed on them for the specific purpose of supporting the New Jersey Public Interest Research Group (PIRG), a group whose aims and views the students opposed, was an infringement of their First Amendment rights.

PIRG is an outside lobbying group, independent of the university, that though nonpartisan actively advocates social change by lobbying for such politically hot items as ERA and a freeze on nuclear weapons. At Rutgers, PIRG was funded through a neutral funding mechanism rather than through the traditional mandatory fee because it was not an on-campus organization. Under this funding mechanism, if the university administration approved the organization's "concept plan," the plan would be put to a vote of the student population at each Rutgers campus. If 25 percent plus one of the student body were to vote to fund the group, a fee would be mandatorily exacted from all students. Students objecting to the collection and use of the fee could then request a refund. PIRG's concept plan received the requisite university and student support in each of three successive years.

In the initial litigation, the district court upheld distribution of the fees to PIRG on the basis of the refund system, which it found to adequately protect students' constitutional rights. On appeal, the Third Circuit reversed the district court, ruling that the refund system did not provide adequate protection of students' rights, and remanded the case to the lower court for determination of whether the allocation of fees to PIRG did indeed violate the objecting students' First Amendment rights. Upon remand, the district court, through extensive findings of fact, determined that distribution of mandatory student fees to PIRG was constitutionally permissible, because PIRG's activities at Rutgers had a "very substantial educational component" that enhanced "the educational opportunities available at that university" *(Galda* 1984, p. 496).

In its second appeal, the most recent installment of the *Galda* saga, the Third Circuit reversed the district court, finding its decision clearly erroneous and the use of the fees to support PIRG unconstitutional. This ruling appears limited in that it applies only to "outside," off-campus organizations and "neutral funding" mechanisms. Indeed:

> . . . *we do not enter the controversy on whether a given* campus organization *may participate in the general activities fee despite the objections of some who are required to contribute to that fund. . . . The question here is limited to . . . an independent outside organization . . .* [emphasis added] *(Galda* 1985, p. 1066).

Even though the legal holding is limited, the court's analysis is similar to that in earlier cases involving mandatory fees and gives the most telling hints as to how other courts will analyze cases concerning mandatory fees and on-campus groups.

The Third Circuit used a two-tier approach to determine that use of mandatory though refundable fees to fund PIRG

If the fee and/ or its use is itself judged unconstitutional . . . changing the method of collection will not make a difference.

is unconstitutional. First, the court ruled that the district court incorrectly found PIRG to serve a substantial educational function. The group's activities were only incidentally related to such educational purposes, and the court concluded PIRG's primary function was political, not educational. Further, other groups on campus directly served the same educational functions PIRG was claiming to fulfill indirectly. Thus, the court held that ". . . the educational component [of PIRG] cannot obscure the underlying substance of the plaintiffs' complaint that they were compelled to finance a political entity whose [primary] function is to attain certain fixed ideological objectives" (*Galda* 1985, p. 1069).

Second, the court found that the university did not meet the "heavy burden" of demonstrating a compelling state interest in supporting PIRG, which would override the complaining students' First Amendment rights. Rather, the court maintained, the educational experience cited as justification for funding PIRG could be gained by other means.

The recent *Galda* decision thus cautions that the primary purpose of a group funded by mandatory fees must be educational and that overriding, compelling state interests must be shown when students' rights are infringed upon to some extent. The ruling likewise indicates that funding to independent, off-campus groups will be treated with much greater scrutiny than funding to on-campus organizations.

The *Galda* opinion also sheds some light on the problems surrounding choice of collection systems. It treats as highly suspect Rutgers's "neutral funding" mechanism, because such a system is directed at one group alone:

> *Generally, when an activity fund comes into existence, all student groups on campus are free to compete for a fair share. That is not the situation here where the mandated contribution is earmarked for only one organization. . . . The objection to funding an outside entity through the "neutral funding" procedure is that the result achieved is not neutral and does not achieve equal access (Galda 1985, p. 1071).*

In addition, the Third Circuit rejected the refund system as providing minimal protection of constitutional rights. The court seemed to support, although through its noncommittal footnote, the check-off or reverse check-off systems "because they allow students to decide in advance if they wish to support PIRG" (p. 1073).

Summary

Funds generated by mandatory fees may be allocated on a prorated basis. While many institutions allow student governments to distribute the funds in any of several methods, courts and institutional policies have recognized the universities' power to intervene when appropriate to prohibit or direct the use of specific funds if campus policy or procedures for allocation have not been followed.

The courts have not upheld religious objections to the use of mandatory fees for abortions, an alleged violation of the free exercise clause, and political objections to the use of mandatory fees for political activity, an alleged violation of the freedoms of association, speech, and expression, have met with mixed results. First, a student's disagreement with the views of one organization was balanced against the institution's need to allow various organizations of conflicting viewpoints to exist and receive funds in order to promote the free exchange of ideas. In these situations, the institution's objectives supersede the individual's rights.

The method of collecting fees that incorporates a pay-back scheme for organizations with which the student disagrees may not be required, according to court rulings, but some institutions have used the method in risk management.

The *Galda* saga leaves one further confused. Although the Third Circuit's current opinion is that funding political action groups like PIRG through mandatory student fees is unconstitutional, the line between these political action groups and other student organizations may not be as clear as the Third Circuit maintains. Further litigation may be necessary to unravel the tangle or to measure the scope of the court's interpretation of what constitutes unconstitutional uses of mandatory fees.

COMMERCIAL SOLICITATION ON CAMPUS

Commercial solicitation is a form of commercial speech, although it is afforded less than the full array of constitutional safeguards for free speech. While the First Amendment does protect "commercial speech" against unwarranted governmental regulation, it can be regulated in a manner not necessarily permissible in the arena of noncommercial or pure speech.

It may be argued that solicitors, if they are outsiders who have no connection with the college or university, have no right to come on campus. The students may have First Amendment rights, the argument would continue, but their rights are not infringed upon by prohibiting outsiders from soliciting. The problem with this argument is that "the First Amendment embraces the right to hear as well as to speak" [*Brooks* v. *Auburn University,* 412 F.2d 1171 (5th Cir. 1969), p. 1172]. By restricting solicitors, therefore, a college could be violating the First Amendment rights of its students even if it were not violating the First Amendment rights of the outsiders.

What are the boundaries of constitutional protection for noncommercial and for commercial speech? How do these protections extend to the college campus?

Noncommercial Speech
The First Amendment right to freedom of speech is not absolute. States may enforce rules restricting the time, place, or manner in which individuals may exercise the freedom of speech. Such regulations may serve to promote order by regulating traffic flow, safeguarding public and private property, and protecting the administration of justice and other basic governmental functions [*Cox* v. *Louisiana,* 379 U.S. 536 (1965)].

To ensure the implementation of free expression, these restrictions must satisfy four requirements, according to the Supreme Court: The restrictions must (1) be content neutral and (2) narrowly drawn, (3) serve a significant governmental interest, and (4) leave open alternative channels of communication [*Perry Education Association* v. *Perry Local Educators Association,* 460 U.S. 37 (1983)]. These requirements, including supplemental considerations like the nature of the restriction and the particular circumstances for which a restriction applies, provide the basis

---

for judicial review of the reasonableness and appropriateness of the restrictions.

Restrictions on time, for example, that limit expression during specific times, promote certain societal interests, such as uninterrupted performance of desirable activities. While regulations governing time, place, or manner must meet the general requirements outlined by the Court, their reasonableness is gauged by the particular circumstances in which they are applied [*Grayned* v. *City of Rockford,* 408 U.S. 104 (1972)]. In *Grayned,* the Supreme Court upheld an antinoise ordinance designed to prevent disruption in the classroom. The ordinance met the Court's requirements, because it applied only while school was in session (p. 120).

Commercial Speech
Commercial speech is expression related solely to the economic interests of the speaker—the solicitor in the context of the college campus—and his audience [*Central Hudson Gas and Electric Corporation* v. *Public Service Commission at New York,* 447 U.S. 557 (1980)]. Commercial expression is entitled to protection under the First Amendment, because the free flow of information is valuable to society [*Virginia State Board of Pharmacy* v. *Virginia Citizens Consumer Council,* 425 U.S. 748 (1976)]. Even so, the Supreme Court has not discarded the "common sense distinction between speech proposing a commercial transaction [that] occurs in an area traditionally subject to government regulation and other varieties of speech" (p. 755). Because commercial speech is viewed differently, it receives a "limited measure of protection commensurate with its subordinate position on the scale of First Amendment values" [*Ohralik* v. *Ohio State Bar Association,* 436 U.S. 447 (1978), p. 456].

In *Ohralik,* the Court considered the constitutionality of a state bar association's restriction mandating the discipline of lawyers who solicit clients *in person* for pecuniary gain. The court labeled the expression in question as "a business transaction in which speech [was] an essential but subordinate component" (p. 457). The element of conduct—solicitation in person—introduced the additional factor of physical activity, which could be regulated even if connected with noncommercial speech. Unlike advertisements, which simply provide information, solicitation in person lends itself to exerting pressure and demanding an immediate response. Moreover, the consumer may not have an opportunity for comparison and reflection.

Regulation of commercial speech is permissible if the speech being prohibited concerns lawful activity and is not misleading. In that case, then the following requirements must be met for a restriction on the speech to be valid: The regulation must directly advance a significant governmental interest, and it must not be more extensive than is necessary to serve that interest *(Central Hudson* 1980). An additional concern often cited, just as in the consideration of regulating noncommercial speech, is whether ample alternative channels are available for the communication of information. Courts have considered newspapers, radio, and mail service as appropriate alternative channels [see *American Future Systems* v. *Pennsylvania State University,* 752 F.2d 854 (3rd Cir. 1984)].

Commercial Speech on Campus

The legal parameters surrounding commercial solicitation on campus became more definitive in a series of legal rulings over six years involving American Future Systems (AFS) and The Pennsylvania State University. At issue were attempts by AFS representatives to demonstrate and sell their products in university residence halls. AFS sells housewares at "shows" hosted by students whom it has called and to whom it has promised gifts for acting as hosts. The student hosts in turn invite other students to the shows, where they are told they might win a four-day vacation in Florida. At the conclusion of the AFS demonstration, the students who do not wish to purchase AFS products are asked to leave, and the remaining students are asked to sign consumer finance contracts.

Finding its demonstrations prohibited or severely restricted by dormitory regulations at Penn State, AFS raised a First Amendment challenge to the university's authority. In *American Future Systems* v. *Pennsylvania State University* [464 F. Supp. 1252 (M.D. Pa. 1979); *aff'd,* 618 F.2d 252 (3rd Cir. 1980)] (hereafter, "AFS1"), Penn State prohibited all commercial transactions in the dormitories, except when an individual student had invited a salesperson to his or her room "for the purpose of transacting business with that student only" (AFS1 1980, p. 254). The regulations did not preclude the placing of advertisements in the student newspaper or on the student radio station, nor did they prohibit sales attempts by phone or mail. While AFS representatives could demonstrate their products to groups of students in the residence halls, they could consummate sales only in the rooms of individual students who had invited them. The Third Circuit Court of Appeals recognized that Penn State had a substantial interest in preserving the proper atmosphere for study and the privacy of students and that the university had restricted commercial speech somewhat, although appropriate within the circumstances. Penn State's regulations thus survived this initial attack by AFS.

In *American Future Systems* v. *Pennsylvania State University* [552 F. Supp. 554 (M.D. Pa. 1981); 688 F.2d 907 (3rd Cir. 1982)]—hereafter "AFS2"—Penn State rejected a proposal by AFS to conduct group demonstrations in individual student's rooms, with the actual consummation of sales occurring in the purchaser's room on a one-on-one basis. AFS then forwarded to Penn State the printed text of the presentation it sought to make in the common rooms of the residence halls. The university refused to permit AFS to include in the group presentation any information about price, guarantees, or payment plan. AFS responded by seeking a court order allowing it to make uncensored group presentations "in the common areas of the residence halls upon invitation by a resident student and to consummate sales on a one-on-one basis with a student who has invited an AFS representative back to his or her private dormitory room" (AFS2 1982, p. 911). In remanding the case to the lower court, the Third Circuit held that, although the university had substantial interests in maintaining the proper atmosphere for study and in protecting the privacy of its students, "[r]estrictions on the *contents* of the demonstration cannot further these interests" (p. 913). The court also rejected the student plaintiffs' claim that their constitutional right to privacy included a right to receive visitors and be received as visitors in dormitory rooms.

AFS and several Penn State students renewed their suit, Penn State countered, and both sides appealed again. The conclusion—and the subsequent decision of the court to deny any rehearings of the matter—appears to be in the ruling of *American Future Systems* v. *Pennsylvania State University* [553 F. Supp. 1268 (M.D. Pa. 1982); 568 F. Supp. 666 (1983); *rev'd,* 752 F.2d 854 (3rd Cir. 1984); *cert. denied, Johnson* v. *Pennsylvania State University,* 105 S.Ct. 3537 (1985)] (hereafter "AFS3"). The Third Circuit Court of Appeals held constitutional Penn State's regulation banning group commercial solicitation in its students' dormitory rooms, concluding that the regulation directly advanced the university's substantial interests, as property owner and as educator, in maintaining its dormitories as a residential and study area for its students and in preventing their use as a rent-free merchandise mart and found the regulation not excessive in light of this objective (AFS3 1984, p. 855).

This 1984 ruling held that Penn State's regulation did not unconstitutionally infringe upon the right of students to receive commercial information in association with other students or upon the right of AFS to disseminate such commercial information (AFS3 1984, p. 856). If invited by a student, a commercial vendor may conduct a one-on-one demonstration and sale in that student's own room. In addition, the telephone, mails, student newspaper, and college radio station are all available at Penn State to commercial entities who want to advertise in the student market. Finally, the university's regulation does not prohibit all group solicitation on state-owned property. Penn State makes a facility on campus, the Nittany Lion Inn, available to AFS as well as to other vendors for group sales and demonstrations. Penn State therefore met the *Central Hudson* test for regulating commercial speech in its specific restriction on commercial speech in its dormitory rooms.

If invited by a student, a commercial vendor may conduct a one-on-one demonstration and sale in that student's own room.

Commercial Speech outside Residence Rooms
Other areas of the campus might be susceptible to commercial solicitation because the areas are considered public forums *[Spartacus Youth League* v. *Board of Trustees of Illinois Industrial University,* 502 F. Supp. 789 (N.D. Ill. 1980)]. In *Spartacus,* university regulations prohibited distribution by the plaintiffs of political literature in the student union. Although the district court did not define the exact parameters of commercial speech in that limited public forum, the student union is generally considered the

most appropriate campus forum for commercial expression. It is in the student union that commercial transactions regularly occur, and it is the student union that is typically designed to be the center of the various aspects of student life.

Particularly when commercial vendors are forbidden from all other areas of the campus, a college might be required to make space available to them in the student union to ensure ample opportunity for them to convey their commercial messages. The courts have implied, however, that student newspapers and radio stations provide ample alternative channels for such expression (AFS1 1980). Availability of the student media notwithstanding, a college or university could probably legally justify specific regulations distinguishing between student organizations acting in a commercial capacity (for example, fund raising) and outside commercial vendors soliciting business. Use of space in a student union building by students would comply with the building's essential role as a center of student life in that students' supporting each other's fund-raising activities is often an integral part of the collegiate experience. Regular commercial vendors, conversely, do not serve the student union's purpose as directly as do the institution's student organizations.

Even if space must be made available to outside commercial vendors, the college or university can enforce reasonable regulations, given the limited space available. Space for a specific time, for example, could be allocated according to order of application.

Determining "Reasonable" Regulations

The courts have been consistent in ruling that colleges and universities may prohibit any misleading or unlawful commercial solicitation. A vendor thus could be denied access to the campus if the vendor had attracted business from students by falsely promising them interest-free credit on their purchases (AFS2; AFS3). To justify a restriction for such reasons, however, the college must have proof of its allegations.

In the absence of a justified blanket prohibition or evidence that certain solicitation is misleading or unlawful, a college or university still may restrict the time, place, and manner of commercial solicitation. To determine whether a particular kind of restriction is permissible, it must first be determined whether the school has a genuine interest as an educational institution in imposing restrictions on the solicitation at issue. If so, then it must be determined whether another way of protecting that interest is possible while imposing fewer restrictions on the vendors. If no less restrictive approach is possible, then the proposed restriction would probably be permissible *(Perry Education Association* 1983).

Restrictions must also be enforced consistently so that no single vendor is treated disparately from others. Administrators must make every effort to ensure that prohibitions of any type are clear of arbitrary, capricious, or discriminatory actions.

Summary
Commercial speech, unlike other speech, can be restricted if restriction advances a governmental interest. On campus, a series of cases indicate that an institutional interest to promote an adequate educational environment will be the basis to uphold policies that severely restrict solicitation or commercial speech in residence halls. Such policies are strengthened when the institution provides another location on campus for vendors to conduct group sales and demonstrations.

Restrictions on commercial speech are more susceptible to court scrutiny when they involve areas designated as public forums. While this fact may mean that institutions must open the student union to vendors if other areas are restricted, some courts have implied that student newspapers and radio stations are adequate and ample channels of commercial speech. Certainly, colleges may enforce reasonable regulations based on space available and order of receipt of applications.

EDUCATIONAL MALPRACTICE AND ACADEMIC DEFERENCE

Contractual and fiduciary student-institutional relationships have been implicated in the litigation concerning the issue of legal liability. While the litigation in the area of contracts depends on specific state laws and the terms of the contract between the consumer and the student, a line of novel cases addresses the fiduciary relationship through the issue of educational malpractice. Educational malpractice has implications not only for faculty and academics but also for those student affairs administrators involved in facilitating an environment that encourages students' achievement in developmental tasks. A review of the case law reveals not only an adherence to the concept of academic deference but also sufficient controversy to warrant the need to understand legal concepts and institutional vulnerability were the courts to give educational malpractice the same credence granted to medical malpractice.

A discussion of malpractice theory must consider the application of contract, fraud, and tort theory. The application of malpractice in education generally and recent decisions demonstrate the courts' differentiation of cases involving physical injury and mental injury. The impact of academic deference is used to formulate projections relative to legal rulings involving students and malpractice.

Malpractice Theory
Much of malpractice theory and liability is based on measuring actions against a standard of care a reasonable professional would use in the practice of his trade. One of the most difficult areas involving malpractice is psychotherapy because of the elusiveness of a standard of care and proximate cause of the alleged injury (Hampton 1984). The concept of educational malpractice has similar problems, and it can be instructive to look at malpractice as applied to psychotherapy to understand the theories of malpractice and apply them to educational situations.

Verbal treatment makes it particularly hard to show the relationship between treatment and suggested injury (Hampton 1984). Further, the controversy over method of treatment has made the establishment of a standard of care difficult. Both these traits are common, not only to psychoanalysis but also to the profession of education.

The cause of action under malpractice theory has three legal bases: (1) contract theory, where the practitioner breaches an expressed obligation to use adequate skill and care; (2) fraud theory, where the practitioner attempts to deceive the patient with a proposed treatment; and (3) tort theory, where the practitioner must use acceptable standards of care in the treatment of the patient (Hampton 1984, p. 255). As can be seen from a discussion of the case law on educational malpractice, contract and fraud theory are elusive theories on which to rely (Funston 1981; Tracy 1980). Contract theory might have particular importance at private institutions, and fraud may be an important element in consumer litigation. But tort theory is the clear choice for the most viable chance for success, not only in psychotherapy malpractice but also in educational malpractice.

The requisite elements of tort theory are (1) the existence of a legal duty for the practitioner to operate within a certain standard of care; (2) the practitioner's breach of that standard of care; and (3) the alleged breach as the proximate cause of the injury to the patient (Hampton 1984, p. 256). Both the standard of care and the proximate cause of the injury are difficult issues to satisfy in psychotherapy malpractice and in educational malpractice cases. In psychotherapy, the problem is that nonphysical or verbal treatments make proximate cause of injury difficult to prove. In educational malpractice, the problem is not only the proof of proximate cause but also the proof of injury itself (Funston 1981). Choosing the standard of care to evaluate the practitioner's treatment is another problem. While the standard of care in psychotherapy is difficult to establish, at least some agreement exists that some treatments are unacceptable and that certain minimum procedures can be identified in specific treatments. Few in education agree, however, on what constitutes learning, further exacerbating the problem of establishing a standard of care (Tracy 1980). To understand the concepts of standard of care and proximate cause of injury, it would be appropriate to look at liability cases involving physical injury or a contract.

Liability Involving Physical Injury or a Contract
Because few educational malpractice cases have been brought, it is appropriate to look at other tort and contract claims to understand the concepts of standard of care and proximate cause. Physical injury tort claims and contract

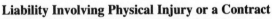

claims demonstrate the application of these theories to potential educational malpractice litigation.

Physical injury
Tort claims in higher education involving personal injury demonstrate not only the standard of care applied in tort cases but also the relationship between the negligence and the injury or proximate cause. One recent example is a case involving a floor hockey game *[Pape* v. *State,* 456 N.Y.S.2d 863 (N.Y. App. Div. 1983)]. A student participant, while attempting to tackle an opponent who had just stolen the puck, suffered a fractured cervical spine. The student sued, alleging that the injury was a direct result of the referee's poor supervision and training. The court found that the referee, in explaining the rules and in refereeing the game, was performing his tasks in a reasonable manner. The plaintiff's own action in attempting an illegal tackle was the proximate cause of his injury.

Another negligence case involved a student who was injured when he slipped and fell in the university's men's locker room *[Van Stry* v. *State,* 479 N.Y.S.2d 258 (N.Y. App. Div. 1984)]. The student was able to show that the pool of water on the locker room floor had been reported to the university on a number of occasions but that the university was negligent in remedying the situation. The court noted that reasonable care was not taken to eliminate the hazard or to warn users of the locker room of the hazard. The proximate cause of the student's injury was the university's failure to take reasonable care.

Another example of institutional negligence is shown in a number of rape cases where a "foreseeable risk" existed to protect students because of a history of criminal activity. *Peterson* v. *San Francisco Community College District* [685 P.2d 1193 (Cal. 1984)], for example, used the standard of a "foreseeable risk." A student was raped on a stairway leading from a parking lot at the college. Other assaults had occurred at that location, but the institution made no attempt to trim the bushes adjacent to the stairway, increase security patrols, or to warn students about the potential danger in that particular parking area. Based on the previous assaults, the institution was negligent in not adequately responding to the "foreseeable risk." In *Miller* v. *State* [478 N.Y.S.2d 829 (N.Y. 1984)], a student raped in her residence hall room also was awarded damages based on "foreseeable risk." The institution had a "reasonably foreseeable" responsibility to secure the building, which was located in a high-crime area and where male intruders had been discovered in the past. *Brown* v. *North Carolina Wesleyan College, Inc.* [309 S.E.2d 701 (N.C. Ct. App. 1983)], however, points to a situation when a "foreseeable risk" did not exist. The institution was not found negligent in a case where a cheerleader was abducted after a basketball game, taken to a rock quarry, raped, and murdered. Because the institution was not located in a high-crime area and campus security measures were adequate under the circumstances, "foreseeable risk" did not exist.

These cases point out the standard of care the institution must observe and the relationship that must exist between the institution's negligence and the injury in establishing proximate cause—standards that must be met in educational malpractice cases. It is the difficulty of establishing the standard and the relationship to proximate cause that has made the theory of educational malpractice tenuous.

Contract liability
Liability claims under contract theory are difficult for plaintiffs to mount if the contract provisions are not clearly spelled out and if the individual is relying on implied agreements. A good case in point is *Sipple* v. *Board of Governors of the University of North Carolina* [318 S.E.2d 256 (N.C. Ct. App. 1984)], in which a faculty member advertised, using stationery with the university's letterhead, a tour to China as a course awarding academic credit. The plaintiff enrolled 15 family members in the course and tour and, according to the faculty member's instructions, mailed a check for $49,000 to a travel agency in California. Subsequently, she received a letter from the faculty member informing her that the tour had been canceled and that the travel agency had gone bankrupt. The plaintiff's suit alleged that the university provided a warranty of reliability for the travel agency. Further, she alleged, an implied contract existed between her and the university, the faculty member had apparent authority to contract for the university, and the university was a surety of the travel agency. The court ruled that the use of university stationery and academic credit did not result in the university's

liability, nor did it make the faculty member a university agent as he had violated university policy by using university stationery. Further, the court said, the plaintiff's direct payment to the travel agency should have indicated to the plaintiff that the tour lacked university endorsement and that the university was not a guarantor of the travel agency's solvency.

This case points out why it might be hard to use implied provisions to establish either an educator's or an institution's obligations to students in malpractice cases. The differences in the interpretation of apparent authority (the official who appears to have the authority to authorize a contractual relationship for the institution) in contract theory between public and private institutions may give greater credence to contractual relationships at private institutions (Hendrickson and Mangum 1977). Apparent authority may make a private institution liable for the actions of its agent, as the plaintiff would have no way of knowing whether the agent has the authority he claims or implies. In public institutions, authority is defined in public statutes or documents, and the plaintiff cannot plead ignorance. Nevertheless, the courts would not necessarily view implied provisions any differently in either sector, particularly when the contract provisions are used to show some professional duty.

These cases all involved negligence resulting in some form of harm to the plaintiff. In educational malpractice cases where mental harm is alleged, the standard of care and proximate cause are much more difficult to discover and prove.

Educational Malpractice

The foundations of educational malpractice have been tested in cases involving elementary and secondary schools. While several suits involved educational malpractice at those levels, only three resulted in reported decisions (Jerry 1981, p. 196). The first malpractice case was *Peter W.* v. *San Francisco Unified School District* [131 Cal. Rptr. 854 (Cal. Ct. App. 1976)]. The student, a high school graduate, sued the district, alleging negligence and misrepresentation. The complaint was based on the fact that he was deficient in both math and reading and in fact possessed the reading skills of an eighth-grade student. He charged that these deficiencies in basic academic skills left him unable to gain employment and rendered him "permanently disabled." Negligence was charged because the teachers failed to provide adequate training in basic academic skills, misrepresentation because the school district had awarded a high school diploma to an individual who could read only at an eighth-grade level. Peter W. contended that the district's alleged negligence in failing to provide him with adequate skills was the proximate cause of his inability to gain employment—the alleged injury. He based his charge of negligence on the assumption that the district's teachers are in a professional relationship with their students and therefore obligated under a legal duty to provide services equal to those used by a reasonably prudent professional.

The California court linked a finding of a legal duty toward the student to public policy and, in rejecting the existence of a professional duty or standard of care for teachers, stated:

> *Unlike the activity of the highway or marketplace, classroom methodology affords no readily acceptable standards of care, or cause, or injury. The science of pedagogy itself is fraught with different and conflicting theories of how or what a child should be taught, and any layman might—and commonly does—have his own emphatic views on the subject. The injury claimed here is plaintiff's inability to read or write. Substantial professional authority attests that the achievement of literacy in the schools, or failure, are [sic] influenced by a host of factors [that] affect the pupil subjectively, from outside the formal teaching process, and beyond the control of its ministers. They may be physical, neurological, emotional, cultural, environmental: they may be present but not perceived, recognized but not identified* (p. 860).

The court questioned not only the necessity for the establishment of a standard of care for teachers but also the ability of the plaintiff to establish a proximate causal relationship between the negligence and the alleged injury. Finally, the court expressed a concern that the establishment of a standard of care for teachers would result in a substantial amount of litigation and create a detrimental burden on the public school system.

In a New York case, *Donohue* v. *Copiague Free School District* [408 N.Y.S.2d 584(N.Y. Sup. Ct. 1977); *aff'd*, 407 N.Y.S.2d 874 (N.Y. App. Div. 1978); *aff'd*, 418 N.Y.S.2d 375 (N.Y. 1979)], the court reached a similar verdict. The plaintiff, a high school graduate who was unable to read or write, alleged that the school had a duty to teach him, to evaluate his learning abilities, and to prescribe effective measures to remediate any deficiencies. Based on this duty, the school was negligent in the supervision of his academic training, and Donohue asked for $5 million in damages. The New York appellate court affirmed the lower court's decision, citing the decision in *Peter W.* but taking a much stronger turn toward the public policy ban to litigation and stating that recognition of a cause of action under educational malpractice would result in the courts' overseeing the management of the public school system, a power clearly reserved by the state's constitution to another branch of government (p. 879). One member of the three-judge panel dissented. In his opinion, this case was no different from medical malpractice cases. The plaintiff's failing grades represented a condition, like an illness, that the teachers as professionals failed to make any attempt to diagnose and treat. Thus, arguments exist for an alternative ruling.

A third case brings the most interesting result [*Hoffman* v. *Board of Education of the City of New York*, 410 N.Y.S.2d 99 (N.Y. App. Div. 1978); *rev'd*, 424 N.Y.S.2d 376 (N.Y. 1979)]. The plaintiff was evaluated at age four as being of normal intelligence even though, immediately after his father's death, Danny suffered speech abnormalities. After entering kindergarten, Danny was given another intelligence test by a school psychologist and diagnosed as possessing borderline intelligence. He was placed in a class with mentally handicapped students. The examining psychologist, while not requesting a past history on Danny before making his diagnosis, recommended that Danny be retested within two years. Danny's mother was never informed of his low intelligence score or her rights to request a reexamination. After attending classes for mentally handicapped individuals for 12 years, Danny was given another intelligence test and found to be of normal intelligence and,

The plaintiff's failing grades represented a condition, like an illness, that the teachers as professionals failed to make any attempt to diagnose and treat.

further, that his learning capacities had always been above average. At trial in a suit against the Board of Education, the jury awarded $750,000 damages to the plaintiff. The New York Appellate Division affirmed the lower court's decision, finding that the failure to retest the student within two years of the original diagnosis, as recommended, constituted neglect. It diminished the award to $500,000, however.

The New York Court of Appeals reversed the appellate court's decision. Citing *Donohue,* the court, in a 4–3 decision, ruled that a cause of action under the concept of educational malpractice could not be considered because it involved public policy beyond the court's purview.

> *. . . There seems little doubt that somewhere there is a suit that can and will be won by an academically injured student. However, at least for the time being, the question has been left for educators to decide. This seems to be the most appropriate place for an educational solution to occur. Courts have emphasized over and over again that these are educational, not legal, questions and as such should be handled by educators* (Patterson 1980, p. 195).

While the case to which the author refers has not yet been found, the position of deference to academicians for academic decisions is a valid point.

Malpractice in Higher Education

Several cases of very recent origin address the question of educational malpractice in higher education. In one case [*Swidryk* v. *St. Michael's Medical Center,* 493 A.2d 641 (N.J. Super. Ct. Law Div. 1985)], an intern, three weeks into his internship at the hospital, was involved in a delivery resulting in brain damage to an infant and a medical malpractice suit against him. He sued the director of medical education for educational malpractice, alleging that the director's failure to adequately supervise the internship and residency programs was the proximate cause of the subsequent medical malpractice suit against the plaintiff. The court, citing *Peter W., Donohue,* and *Hoffman,* used the public policy argument to refuse to allow a cause of action for educational malpractice:

*The legislature has vested the board of medical examin-
ers, the board of higher education, and the advisory
graduate medical education council with the authority to
insure that a proper medical education is delivered
within New Jersey. It would be against public policy for
the court to usurp these functions and inquire into the
day-to-day operation of a graduate medical education
program. From the standpoint of court administration, it
would be unwise to recognize a claim for educational
malpractice where an individual physician is attempting
to defend against a malpractice claim. . . . Therefore,
for reasons of public policy, there is no legal duty [that]
will support a tort for educational malpractice in this
class of case* (p. 645).

While this case does involve questions of medical malpractice, the crux of the plaintiff's allegations centers on the
quality of the supervision and training provided by the
director of medical education.

In a more recent case *[Moore* v. *Vanderloo,* 386 N.W.2d
108 (Iowa 1986)], a patient who suffered a stroke after chi-
ropractic treatment and use of contraceptive devices not
only sued the chiropractor and the contraceptive manufac-
turing company but also filed an educational malpractice
claim against the college from which the chiropractor
received his training and degree. The Supreme Court of
Iowa, citing *Swidryk* among others, used "public policy
considerations" as a basis to dismiss the complaint.

In one other case involving malpractice in higher education *[Bain* v. *Gillispie,* 357 N.W.2d 47 (Iowa Ct. App.
1984)], the court found that a local merchant had no basis
in law for a cause of action for "athletic official's malpractice." A referee brought a defamation of character suit
based on printing on the front of T-shirts a store owner was
selling after a crucial basketball game officiated by that referee. The owner answered with a suit alleging officiating
malpractice in the game.

The Literature on Educational Malpractice
Some have developed cogent legal arguments for the existence of a cause of action for educational malpractice (Collingsworth 1982; Tracy 1980), arguing that a standard of
care can be found, that one can show that educators have a

duty to students, and that proximate cause can be shown between teachers' negligence and alleged learning deficiencies. One author also argued that damages could be limited to remediating those deficiencies (Tracy 1980).

A report on the current status of educational malpractice cases used the literature on teacher education to establish standards of performance, noting that tort law is not static (Clear 1983). A risk management program for the profession, including self-regulation, would negate the need for courts to apply educational malpractice, however (Patterson 1980). Several other recent articles on the subject take a position close to the courts' public policy argument.

> *The theoretical inconsistencies inherent in the principle that no cause of action exists for educational malpractice do not prove that the special policy objectives of the principle are not meritorious. In other words, questioning the logic of the courts' analysis is not the equivalent to questioning the view that our educational system is more viable if the cause of action is not recognized* (Jerry 1981, p. 211).

The legislature will have to make the final decision on whether educational malpractice is a legal tort (Jerry 1981).

This brief review of the litigation and literature on educational malpractice points out the courts' current position that it is not a valid cause of action and demonstrates the viability of arguments for the establishment of educational malpractice as a tort. That position is not inconsistent with the courts' traditional position of academic deference in matters involving educational decisions in higher education.

Academic Dismissal as Proof of Deference
The courts' position of deferring to academicians in academic decision making lends support to the courts' position in educational malpractice. An analysis of decisions in the area of academic dismissal gives credence to the premise of the courts' refusal to become involved in academic decisions. [While a detailed analysis of faculty employment issues also supports the position of deference, it is outside the purview of this monograph (see Hendrickson and Lee 1983).]

In the area of academic dismissal, two types of cases emerge. One group of cases involves dismissal for cheating or plagiarism. These cases, while involving academic issues, also implicate a liberty interest (one's good name or reputation), therefore requiring the due process guaranteed to students enrolled in public institutions. In *Crook* v. *Baker* [584 F. Supp. 1531 (E.D. Mich. 1984)], a student whose degree was removed without due process for the alleged use of fraudulent data in his thesis was found by the court to possess both a liberty and a property interest requiring due process before the degree could be rescinded. Where a liberty or property interest can be legitimately claimed, the courts show no reluctance to step in and insist on the enforcement of constitutionally protected procedures *[Jones* v. *Board of Governors of University of North Carolina,* 704 F.2d 713 (4th Cir. 1983)].

On the other hand, the courts are most reluctant to get involved in cases involving the evaluation of a student's performance or qualifications in the award of grades, credits, or a degree, and *Horowitz* is still controlling in this area. Subsequent cases uphold the position in *Horowitz* of academic deference unless the school has acted in bad faith or in an arbitrary and capricious manner or placed a stigma on the plaintiff's reputation. Failure in a program was not a stigma in *Greenhill* v. *Bailey* [519 F.2d 5 (8th Cir. 1975)]. In *Hines* v. *Rinker* [667 F.2d 699 (8th Cir. 1981)], the court ruled that the evaluation of medical students' performance is a matter for the faculty and not the courts. A number of state courts arrived at similar conclusions *[Patti Ann H.* v. *New York Medical College,* 453 N.Y.S.2d 196 (N.Y. 1982); *Neel* v. *I.U. Board of Trustees,* 435 N.E.2d 607 (Ind. Ct. App. 1982)]. In *Woodruff* v. *Georgia State University* [304 S.E.2d 697 (Ga. 1983)], the court found that disputes involving academic matters should not be subjected to judicial scrutiny but that the student can prevail when it can be shown that the institution operated arbitrarily. In *Ewing* v. *Board of Regents of the University of Michigan* [742 F.2d 913 (6th Cir. 1984)], the student alleged that the institution's refusal to allow him to retake a test a second time, a common practice for the particular testing program, was an arbitrary decision violating the student's property interest and resulting in his dismissal. While the Circuit Court agreed, the Supreme Court overturned its decision. In

Regents of the University of Michigan v. *Ewing* [106 S.Ct. 507 (1985)], the Court found that the university had used adequate professional judgment in evaluating both previous academic performance and the performance on the first test as the basis for a refusal to retake the test.

> *The record unmistakenly demonstrates . . . that the faculty's decision was made conscientiously and with careful deliberation, based on an evaluation of the entirety of Ewing's academic career. When judges are asked to review the substance of a genuinely academic decision, such as this one, they should show great respect for the faculty's professional judgment. Plainly they may not override it unless it is such a substantial departure from accepted academic norms as to demonstrate that the person or committee responsible did not actually exercise professional judgment* (p. 513).

This case gives additional strength to the position of deference and the courts' unwillingness to become involved in academic decisions. While the courts will not tolerate arbitrariness, it is obvious they continue to grant considerable deference to academicians. Because academic decisions and practice are at the heart of educational malpractice cases, this position by the courts of academic deference in academic decision making forms a significant barrier to the application of malpractice theory in higher education.

Summary
A novel area of litigation involving the student as consumer is the relatively new concept of educational malpractice, based on the existence of a legal duty administrators and teachers have in their relationship with students, a standard of care that can be clearly defined, a proximate causal relationship between the negligent practices of the educator and the alleged injury to the student, and verifiable injury. The courts, taking a position of noninterference in academic matters, view educational matters as within the realm of other governmental agencies and therefore, based on sound public policy, beyond adjudication. The courts find it difficult to establish the proximate causal relationship between a teacher's actions and alleged injury to the student; therefore, educational malpractice is not yet a

valid cause for action. This position is consistent with the case law on academic dismissal and faculty employment in higher education. Although tort law changes, that position is not likely to change soon.

IMPLICATIONS FOR POLICY AND PRACTICE

This monograph has traced the historical development of four student-institutional relationships—in loco parentis, fiduciary, contractual, and constitutional. As the case law affected those relationships, fiduciary and contractual relationships superseded in loco parentis as describing students as consumers, and the newer constitutional relationship emerged. As these relationships have changed and as emphasis has moved from one relationship to another, institutional policy must change to reduce the risk of litigation and achieve institutional compliance with the law. The novel litigation in the constitutional and consumer areas is the locus of changes in policy and practice.

The novel litigation in the constitutional and consumer areas changes in policy and practice.

Litigation involving the constitutional relationship has evolved from one emphasizing individual rights in the 1960s and 1970s to First Amendment rights of association and freedom of religion as they affect student organizations in the late 1970s and 1980s. In the last several years, another First Amendment issue involving commercial speech has also been defined.

Issues involving contractual and fiduciary relationships have been litigated as torts based on negligence, breach of contract, or educational malpractice, and the novel consumer litigation lies in the area of educational malpractice. Consumer protection has become more important than in the past, and colleges find themselves struggling to design policies that are consumer focused and, at the same time, preserve past policies that enhance their primary mission.

The Evolution of Constitutional Rights

Through *Dixon,* the Fourteenth Amendment becomes the vehicle to define the constitutional rights students have at public institutions. While the proscriptions defined in *Dixon* are still valid, the rigidity and conformity to strict judicial requirements evident in some literature of the 1970s went beyond the rights defined in that landmark case. Recent literature and case law *(Henson,* for example) reflect a more flexible definition of due process that can accommodate educational objectives while protecting a student's rights.

Litigation in the 1960s and 1970s defined other rights courts have awarded to students. Students' rights of privacy in institutional residence halls were balanced against those of the institution as a landlord and a guardian of the educational environment. Freedom of speech, assembly, and association covered speakers and editorial content of student publications. Only pronouncements that result in disruption or violence, inhibit the rights of others, or are obscene may be stifled; however, the burden of proof lies with the institution to substantiate the existence of any such results.

Rights of due process were not applied to academic dismissal decisions in the 1970s. In fact, the courts have a long history of refusing to become involved in academic decisions, a position that appears to have strengthened over time. Plagiarism and cheating are not viewed as causes for academic dismissals, because they involve a "liberty interest" (one's good name or reputation) requiring due process similar to disciplinary dismissals.

First Amendment Policy Considerations
Recognition of organizations and use of facilities
Administrators of public colleges and universities are bound by the First and Fourteenth Amendments to ensure that rights and privileges are extended to *all* student groups equally and fairly. Administrators of private colleges, while not bound legally by constitutional considerations, may find less conflict acknowledging rights and freedoms required of public colleges by the Constitution, particularly at this time, when American society places a great deal of importance on those rights.

While speech-related activities of student organizations are constitutionally protected, they are subject, however, to some regulation as a result of the special characteristics of the school environment. The Supreme Court, in *Tinker* v. *Des Moines Independent Community School District* [393 U.S. 503 (1969)], made that point clear:

> *Conduct by students, in class or out of it, [that] for any reason—whether it stems from time, place, or type of behavior—materially disrupts classwork or involves substantial disorder or invasion of the rights of others, is, of course, not immunized by the constitutional guarantee of freedom of speech* (p. 513).

Regulations involving student organizations, their recognition, and their use of facilities should be directed toward promoting the educational mission of the college or university, protecting the freedom of speech and rights of association of *all* students, and preventing violence, disruption of the institution's programs, and violations of established laws. Most of all, administrators must make every effort to ensure that student organizations are treated *equally*. Institutional policies and procedures must be directed toward fair play and equality in dealing with students and student organizations.

In sum, while balancing the constitutional rights of students and the prerogatives of the institution, administrators must ensure that:

- Freedom of *speech* is guaranteed, but *behavior* is subject to regulation.
- Behavior that interferes with or disrupts the normal activities of the institution or the rights of others is subject to regulation.
- Regulation of time, place, and manner is lawful for maintaining the proper educational environment of the college or university.
- Once some groups or organizations have been recognized by the institution, *all* groups must be accorded such status, provided they meet the same lawful procedural and substantive requirements.
- Religious speech must be treated as secular speech as it relates to recognition of student organizations and policies regarding the use of institutional facilities.

Collection and use of mandatory student fees
The legal rulings involving mandatory student activity fees make clear that such fees are constitutionally permissible as long as they do not unduly infringe on students' constitutional rights. The courts have also said that, even if some rights are violated, the fees will be upheld if the college or university can demonstrate a compelling state interest in having the use of that particular fee. Such a demonstration will be scrutinized very closely, however. These propositions aside, a large unknown area exists within which administrators can at best use inferences drawn from court rulings to make reasoned judgments about what is and what is not legally permissible.

College administrators should thus structure fee systems to ensure the presence of as many of the following characteristics as possible:

- The group receiving funds is an institutionally dependent, on-campus organization.
- The primary purpose or activity of the group receiving funds is educational—not political—and the group permits expression of a wide range of views.
- The funding mechanism is one to which all on-campus groups have equal access.
- The fee system allows a maximum amount of discussion, approval, or objection by students at the outset, before fees are ever exacted.
- The institutional student activity fee must support a broad forum of ideas and activities, while not promoting or hindering expression of any particular view.

A check-off or reverse check-off system appears to garner the most support from the courts.

It is unlikely that an absence of any one of these characteristics will make a mandatory fee system stand or fall. Absent clear direction from the courts on the issue and a controlling Supreme Court decision, however, implementation of a fee system with as many of these guidelines as possible is likely to be the best course for avoiding legitimate disruptive student dissent and costly, time-consuming litigation.

Commercial speech

Colleges and universities have a substantial interest in providing an environment conducive to implementing their educational goals and in protecting the safety and privacy of their students. Thus, the courts view favorably policies governing commercial speech designed with these criteria as a basis.

Commercial solicitation, a form of commercial speech, is accorded less than the full array of rights guaranteeing free speech, but any restrictive policies must be content neutral and free of arbitrary or capricious action, and nondiscriminatory in application. The courts have ruled further that:

- Administrators may ban group commercial solicitation in students' residence hall rooms.

- College officials are well advised to prevent the use of residence hall rooms as merchandising marts by commercial vendors.
- A one-on-one demonstration and/or sale in a student's private room may be allowed *if the student invites the solicitor.*
- Institutions should provide some means for allowing commercial speech, information, and expression, including newspapers, mail, radio stations, and telephone, for example.
- Colleges and universities may prohibit any misleading or unlawful commercial activity.

Malpractice Policy
Given the current disposition of the courts and the existing overload of cases most courts face, it may be difficult to imagine the expansion of tort law into the area of educational malpractice (although some made the same prediction with regard to students' constitutional rights in 1961). The courts have consistently upheld the concept of deference to academicians in academic matters, and it would behoove faculty and administrators to review policy and practices. Several policy considerations seem appropriate:

- The process for peer review and evaluation by department heads and supervisory administrators should be reviewed to ensure that incompetence and poor performance are not swept under the rug.
- Institutions should ensure that diagnostic procedures meet the practices and procedures accepted by professionals in the field when such standards are available. For example, standardized tests should be used within the guidelines provided by the test authors and with other recommended diagnostic tools.
- Review should be built into the process of awarding grades and certifying skills to protect against arbitrary and capricious decisions and, at the same time, to protect the academic integrity of the faculty evaluation process.
- Catalogs, bulletins, and other publications should be reviewed to ensure that they do not make guarantees beyond the institution's capabilities.

- When controversies develop, institutions should explore options—remediation, for example—that might in the long run avoid costly litigation.

Institutions that approach the question of malpractice with an emphasis on an ethical sense of their obligations to students either will avoid litigation or will find the courts unwilling to intercede.

A Final Word
This monograph has presented implications for policy and practice to assist administrators and faculty in their efforts to understand the application of recent case law on students' rights and institutions' obligations. The law continues to evolve, however, and one may not be wholly able to anticipate changes or avoid suit. The best defense is to identify the ethical, legal, reasonable, and stated obligations to students and to adjust policies and practices to meet those obligations. This approach, allowing administrators to show that they have acted in a reasonable manner under the circumstances, should be defensible in court. This monograph should not, however, be construed as a substitute for the appropriate advice of legal counsel.

REFERENCES

The ERIC Clearinghouse on Higher Education abstracts and indexes the current literature on higher education for the Office of Educational Research and Improvement's monthly bibliographic journal, *Resources in Education*. Most of these publications are available through the ERIC Document Reproduction Service (EDRS). For publications cited in this bibliography that are available from EDRS, ordering number and price are included. Readers who wish to order a publication should write to the ERIC Document Reproduction Service, 3900 Wheeler Avenue, Alexandria, Virginia 22304. When ordering, please specify the document number. Documents are available as noted in microfiche (MF) and paper copy (PC). Because prices are subject to change, it is advisable to check the latest issue of *Resources in Education* for current cost based on the number of pages in the publication.

Books and Periodicals

Aaron, R. M. 1985. "Public Interest Research Groups: Funding Practices on College Campuses." *Journal of College Student Personnel* 26 (4): 322–28.

Alexander, K., and Solomon, E. S. 1972. *College and University Law*. Charlottesville, Va.: Michie Co.

Anderson, Jonathan W. 1981. "The Constitutional Rights of College Students to Use State-Owned University Buildings for Religious Purposes." *Notre Dame Lawyer* 57 (1): 91–111.

Baier, Beth K. 1983. "Student Refusal to Pay Abortion-Related Fees—A First Amendment Right?" *San Diego Law Review* 20 (4): 837–57.

Bauer, Janine G. 1983. "The Constitutionality of Student Fees for Political Student Groups in the Campus Public Forum: *Galda* v. *Bloustein* and the Right to Associate." *Rutgers Law Journal* 15 (1): 135–85.

Bean, Sheila J., and Hines, Edward R. 1981. "The Student-Institutional Relationship: Contract Provisions and Consumer Protection." *Journal of College Student Personnel* 22 (1): 36–41.

Biemiller, Lawrence. 7 August 1985. "Homosexual Groups at Georgetown U. Get Court Backing." *Chronicle of Higher Education* 30 (23): 1+.

Black, Henry Campbell. 1979. *Black's Law Dictionary*. 5th ed. St. Paul, Minn.: West Publishing Co.

Brittain, K. 1971. "Colleges and Universities: The Demise of *In Loco Parentis*." *Land and Water Law Review* 6: 727–30.

Campbell, Richard W. 1982. "*Widmar* v. *Vincent:* The Protection of Religious Speech in the Public University." *Ohio Northern University Law Review* 9 (3): 503–10.

Chambers, M. M. 1976. *The College and the Courts: The Developing Law of the Student and the College*. Normal, Ill.: Illinois State University. ED 130 580. 65 pp. MF–$1.00; PC–$7.29.

Chronicle of Higher Education. 23 October 1985. "Georgetown U.'s Refusal to Recognize Homosexual Groups Goes to Appeals Court" 31 (8): 3.

Clear, Delbert. 1983. "Malpractice in Teacher Education: The Improbable Becomes Increasingly Possible." *Journal of Teacher Education* 24 (2): 19–24.

Collingsworth, Terrance P. 1982. "Applying Negligence to the Teaching Profession." *Journal of Law and Education* 11 (4): 479–505.

Conrath, Richard C. 1976. "In Loco Parentis: Recent Developments in This Legal Doctrine as Applied to the Student-Institutional Relationship in the United States of America, 1965–1975." Doctoral dissertation, Kent State University. ED 136 672. 203 pp. MF–$1.00; PC–$18.81.

DeGuisti, Stephen L. 1982. "Constitutional Law: *Widmar* v. *Vincent*—A Departure from the Traditional Approach to Cases Involving Religion and Education." *Oklahoma Law Review* 35 (3): 604–15.

Diener, Thomas J., ed. 1971. "The Law and Higher Education: Where the Action Is." Proceedings of a conference on higher education and the law. Tuscaloosa: University of Alabama. ED 056 642. 39 pp. MF–$1.00; PC–$5.44.

Edwards, Harry T., and Nordin, Virginia Davis. 1979. *Higher Education and the Law*. Cambridge, Mass.: Institute for Educational Management.

———. 1983. *Higher Education and the Law: Cumulative Supplement*. Cambridge, Mass.: Institute for Educational Management.

El-Khawas, Elaine. 1979. "To Assure Fair Practice toward Students." *Educational Record* 60: 282–94.

Funston, Richard. 1981. "Educational Malpractice: A Cause of Action in Search of a Theory." *San Diego Law Review* 18 (5): 743–812.

Gibbs, Annette. 1979. "Gay Student Organizations on Campus: The Controversy Continues." *Journal of College Student Personnel* 20 (6): 485–89.

———. 1980. "Mandatory Student Activity Fees: Educational and Legal Considerations." *Journal of College Student Personnel* 21 (6): 535–40.

———. 1984. "Colleges and Gay Student Organizations: An Update." *NASPA Journal* 22 (1): 38–42.

———. 1986. "Solicitation on Campus: Free Speech or Commercialization?" *Journal of College Student Personnel* 27 (1): 49–53.

Gibbs, Annette, and Jernigan, Miriam. 1980. "Commercial Activity on Campus: Where Does It End?" *NASPA Journal* 18 (1): 28–33.

Gibbs, Annette, and Kennedy, Ann. 1986. "Freedom of Religion and the State University's Use of Mandatory Student Fees for Abortion-Related Expenses." Unpublished manuscript.

Hampton, Lawrence P. 1984. "Malpractice in Psychotherapy: Is There a Relevant Standard of Care?" *Case Western Reserve Law Review* 35: 251–81.

Harms, Herman Edward. 1970. *The Concept of In Loco Parentis in Higher Education.* ERIC Clearinghouse on Higher Education. ED 042 421. 34 pp. MF–$1.00; PC–$5.44.

Hendrickson, Robert M., and Lee, Barbara A. 1983. *Academic Employment and Retrenchment: Judicial Review and Administrative Action.* ASHE-ERIC Higher Education Research Report No. 8. Washington, D.C.: Association for the Study of Higher Education. ED 290 972. 133 pp. MF–$1.00; PC–$12.84.

Hendrickson, Robert M., and Mangum, Ronald Scott. 1977. *Governing Board and Administrator Liability.* AAHE-ERIC Higher Education Research Report No. 9. Washington, D.C.: American Association for Higher Education. ED 148 256. 72 pp. MF–$1.00; PC–$7.29.

Henry, David D. 1975. *Challenges Past, Challenges Present.* San Francisco: Jossey-Bass.

Hobbs, Walter C. 1981. "The Courts." In *Higher Education in American Society,* edited by Philip G. Altbach and Robert O. Berdahl. Buffalo: Prometheus Books.

———, ed. 1978. *Government Regulation of Higher Education.* Cambridge, Mass.: Ballinger Publishing Co.

Hollander, Patricia A.; Young, D. P.; and Gehring, D. D. 1985. *A Practical Guide for Legal Issues Affecting College Teachers.* Asheville, N.C.: College Administration Publications.

Howarth, Don, and Connell, William D. 1981. "Students' Rights to Organize and Meet for Religious Purposes in the University Context." *Valparaiso University Law Review* 16 (1): 103–43.

Jerry, Robert H. 1981. "Recovery in Tort for Educational Malpractice: Problems of Theory and Policy." *Kansas Law Review* 29: 195–212.

Johnson, D. 1971. "In Loco Parentis and Political Attitudes: Their Relationship as Viewed by Eight University of Oregon Publics." Doctoral dissertation, University of Oregon.

Kaplin, William A. 1979. *The Law of Higher Education.* San Francisco: Jossey-Bass.

————. 1985. *The Law of Higher Education*. 2d ed. San Francisco: Jossey-Bass.

Kemerer, Frank R., and Deutsch, Kenneth L. 1979. *Constitutional Rights and Student Life*. St. Paul, Minn.: West Publishing Co.

Lauren, Jason F. 1984. " 'Fee Speech': First Amendment Limitations on Student Fee Expenditures." *California Western Law Review* 20 (2): 279–311.

Lerblance, Penn. 1979. "Legal and Educational Aspects of Student Dismissal." *Southwestern Law Journal* 33 (2): 605–33.

Long, Nicholas Trott. 1985. "The Standard of Proof in Student Disciplinary Cases." *Journal of College and University Law* 12 (1): 71–81.

Meaborn, David; Suddick, David; and Gibbs, Annette. 1985. *A Student Activity Fee Primer: Current Research on Collection, Control, and Allocation*. Columbia, S.C.: National Association for Campus Activities.

Millington, William G. 1979. *The Law and the College Student*. St. Paul, Minn.: West Publishing Co.

Minker, Debra G. 1983. "Constitutional Law—First Amendment: *Widmar* v. *Vincent*." *Emory Law Journal* 32 (1): 319–48.

Morton, Susan E. 1985. "Who Should Speak? Who Should Pay? The Complexities of Refunding Student Fees at Public Colleges and Universities." *Journal of College and University Law* 11 (4): 481–500.

Newell, Lisa M. 1982–83. "Use of Campus Facilities for First Amendment Activity." *Journal of College and University Law* 9 (1): 27–39.

Nordin, Virginia D. 1982. "The Contract to Educate: Toward a More Workable Theory of the Student-Institutional Relationship." *Journal of College and University Law* 8 (2): 141–81.

Note. 1983. "Time, Place, or Manner Restrictions on Commercial Speech." *George Washington Law Review* 52 (1): 28–33.

Ostroth, D. David, and Hill, David E. 1978. "The Helping Relationship in Student Discipline." *The NASPA Journal* 6 (2): 33–39.

Patterson, Arlene H. 1980. "Professional Malpractice: Small Cloud, but Growing Bigger." *Phi Delta Kappan* 62 (3): 193–96.

Serra, J. 1968. "In Loco Parentis: A Survey of Attitudes of Parents of Undergraduate Students." Doctoral dissertation, Indiana University.

Stanley, William R. 1983–84. "The Rights of Gay Student Organizations." *Journal of College and University Law* 10 (3): 397–418.

Stark, Joan S., ed. 1976. *Promoting Consumer Protection for Students*. New Directions for Higher Education No. 13. San Francisco: Jossey-Bass.

Tracy, Destin Shane. 1980. "Educational Negligence: A Student's Cause of Action for Incompetent Academic Instruction." *North Carolina Law Review* 58: 561–97.

Van Alstyne, William. 1962. "Procedural Due Process and State University Students." *U.C.L.A. Law Review* 10: 378.

———. 1965. "Student Academic Freedom and the Role-Making Powers of Public Universities: Some Constitutional Considerations." *Law in Transition Quarterly* 2: 3.

———. 1968a. "Judicial Trends toward Student Academic Freedom." *University of Florida Law Review* 20: 290–301.

———. 1968b. "The Student as University Resident." *Denver Law Journal* 45: 591.

Wagoner, Jennings, Jr. 1968. "From In Loco Parentis toward *Lernfrehidt:* An Explanation of the Attitudes of Four Early Presidents Regarding Student Freedom and Character Development." Doctoral dissertation, Ohio State University.

Willamette Law Journal. 1979. *"Board of Curators of the University of Missouri* v. *Horowitz:* Student Due Process Rights and Judicial Deference to Academic Dismissal" 15 (3): 577–91.

Winn, S. Ezra. 1982. "Recent Developments—Religious Activities in State Universities." *Tennessee Law Review* 49 (3): 623–51.

Young, D. Parker. 1973. *Ramifications of the Age of Majority*. Detroit: COSPA. ED 125 482. 18 pp. MF–$1.00; PC–$3.59.

———. 1976. *The Law and the Student in Higher Education*. Athens, Ga.: National Organization on Legal Problems of Education.

Cases and Statutes
Student-institutional relationships

Anthoney v. *Syracuse University,* 231 N.Y.S. 435 (N.Y. App. Div. 1928).

Board of Curators of the University of Missouri v. *Horowitz,* 435 U.S. 78 (1978).

Buttney v. *Smiley,* 281 F. Supp. 280 (D. Colo. 1968).

Carr v. *St. Johns University,* 231 N.Y.S.2d 403 (N.Y. App. Div. 1962); *aff'd,* 235 N.Y.S.2d 834 (N.Y. 1962).

Dixon v. *Alabama,* 294 F.2d 150 (5th Cir. 1961); *cert. denied,* 286 U.S. 930 (1961).

Evans v. *State Board of Agriculture,* 325 F. Supp. 1353 (E.D. Colo. 1971).

Gott v. *Berea College,* 161 S.W. 204 (Ky. 1913).

Healy v. *Larsson*, 323 N.Y.S.2d 625 (N.Y. Sup. Ct. 1971); *aff'd*, 348 N.Y.S.2d 971 (N.Y. App. Div. 1971); *aff'd*, 360 N.Y.S.2d 419 (N.Y. 1974).

Moore v. *Student Affairs Committee of Troy State University*, 284 F. Supp. 725 (M.D. Ala. 1968).

Soglin v. *Kauffman*, 295 F. Supp. 978 (W.D. Wis. 1968).

Steier v. *New York State Education Commission*, 271 F.2d 150 (5th Cir. 1959).

Evolution of constitutional rights

Antonelli v. *Hammond*, 308 F. Supp. 1329 (D. Mass. 1970).

Barker v. *Hardway*, 283 F. Supp. 228 (S.D. W.Va. 1968).

Bayless v. *Maritime*, 430 F.2d 873 (5th Cir. 1970).

Board of Curators of the University of Missouri v. *Horowitz*, 435 U.S. 78 (1978).

Buttney v. *Smiley*, 281 F. Supp. 280 (D. Colo. 1968).

Chess v. *Widmar*, 635 F.2d 1310 (8th Cir. 1980); *aff'd, Widmar* v. *Vincent*, 454 U.S. 263 (1981).

Crook v. *Baker*, 584 F. Supp. 1531 (E.D. Mich. 1984).

Dickey v. *Alabama*, 273 F. Supp. 613 (M.D. Ala. 1967).

Dixon v. *Alabama*, 294 F.2d 150 (5th Cir. 1961); *cert. denied*, 286 U.S. 930 (1961).

Esteban v. *Central Missouri State College*, 277 F. Supp. 649 (W.D. Mo. 1967).

Family Educational Rights and Privacy Act of 1974, 41 CFR 9062 (1976).

French v. *Bashful*, 303 F. Supp. 1333 (E.D. La. 1969).

Gay Liberation v. *University of Missouri*, 558 F.2d 848 (8th Cir. 1977).

Gay Students Organization of the University of New Hampshire v. *Bonner*, 367 F. Supp. 1088 (D. N.H. 1974); *aff'd*, 509 F.2d 652 (1st Cir. 1974).

Griswold v. *Connecticut*, 381 U.S. 479 (1965).

Gross v. *Lopez*, 419 U.S. 565 (1975).

Grove City College v. *Bell*, 104 S.Ct. 1211 (1984).

Hammond v. *South Carolina State College*, 272 F. Supp. 947 (D. S.C. 1967).

Healy v. *James*, 408 U.S. 169 (1972).

Henson v. *Honor Committee of the University of Virginia*, 719 F.2d 69 (4th Cir. 1983).

Jenkins v. *Louisiana State Board of Education*, 506 F.2d 992 (5th Cir. 1975).

Joyner v. *Whiting*, 477 F.2d 456 (4th Cir. 1973).

Moore v. *Student Affairs Committee of Troy State University*, 284 F. Supp. 725 (M.D. Ala. 1968).

North Haven v. *Bell,* 456 U.S. 509 (1982).
Papish v. *Board of Curators of the University of Missouri,* 410 U.S. 667 (1972).
Piazzola v. *Watkins,* 442 F. Supp. 284 (5th Cir. 1971).
Regents of the University of Michigan v. *Ewing,* 106 S.Ct. 507 (1985).
Rehabilitation Act of 1973, 29 U.S.C. 701.
Southeastern Community College v. *Davis,* 442 U.S. 397 (1979).
Speakes v. *Grantham,* 317 F. Supp. 1253 (S.D. Miss. 1970).
Stacy v. *Williams,* 306 F. Supp. 963 (N.D. Miss. 1969).
Tinker v. *Des Moines Independent Community School District,* 393 U.S. 503 (1969).
Title VI of the Civil Rights Act of 1964, 42 U.S.C. 2000(d), *et seq.* (1978).
Title VII of the Civil Rights Act of 1964, 42 U.S.C. 2000(e), *et seq.* (1978).
Title IX of the Education Amendments of 1972, 20 U.S.C. 1681.
Tully v. *Orr,* 608 F. Supp. 1222 (E.D. N.Y. 1985).
Wright v. *Texas Southern University,* 392 F.2d 728 (5th Cir. 1968).

Recognition and use of facilities
Bob Jones University v. *United States,* 461 U.S. 574 (1983).
Chess v. *Widmar,* 480 F. Supp. 907 (W.D. Mo. 1979); *rev'd,* 635 F.2d 1310 (8th Cir. 1980).
Chess v. *Widmar,* 635 F.2d 1310 (8th Cir. 1980); *aff'd, Widmar* v. *Vincent,* 454 U.S. 263 (1981).
Everson v. *Board of Education,* 330 U.S. 1 (1947).
Gay Activists Alliance v. *Board of Regents of University of Oklahoma,* 638 P.2d 1116 (Okla. 1981).
Gay Rights Coalition v. *Georgetown University,* 496 A.2d 567 (D.C. Cir. 1985), *vacated* and *reh'g granted,* 496 A.2d 587 (D.C. Cir. 1985).
Gay Student Services v. *Texas A&M University,* 737 F.2d 1317 (5th Cir. 1984); *reh'g denied,* 105 S.Ct. 1860 (1985).
Gay Students Organization of the University of New Hampshire v. *Bonner,* 367 F. Supp. 1088 (D. N.H. 1974); *aff'd,* 509 F.2d 652 (1st Cir. 1974).
Grayned v. *City of Rockford,* 408 U.S. 104 (1972).
Healy v. *James,* 408 U.S. 169 (1972).
Perry Education Association v. *Perry Local Educators Association,* 460 U.S. 37 (1983).
Police Department v. *Mosley,* 408 U.S. 92 (1972).
Student Coalition for Gay Rights v. *Austin Peay State University,* 477 F. Supp. 1267 (M.D. Tenn. 1979).

Tinker v. *Des Moines Independent Community School District,* 393 U.S. 503 (1969).

Widmar v. *Vincent,* 454 U.S. 263 (1981).

Wood v. *Davison,* 351 F. Supp. 543 (N.D. Ga. 1972).

Zorach v. *Clauson,* 343 U.S. 306 (1952).

Mandatory student fees: Collection and use

Abood v. *Detroit Board of Education,* 431 U.S. 209 (1977).

Associated Students, San Jose State University v. *Trustees of California State Universities and Colleges,* 128 Cal. Rptr. 601 (Cal. Ct. App. 1976).

Erzinger v. *Regents of the University of California,* 187 Cal. Rptr. 164 (Cal. Ct. App. 1982).

Galda v. *Bloustein,* 686 F.2d 159 (3rd Cir. 1982).

Galda v. *Rutgers,* 589 F. Supp. 479 (D. N.J. 1984); *rev'd* and *remanded,* 772 F.2d 1060 (3rd Cir. 1985).

Good v. *Associated Students, University of Washington,* 542 P.2d 762 (Wash. 1975).

Kentucky Educators Public Affairs Council v. *Kentucky Registry of Election Finance,* 677 F.2d 1125 (6th Cir. 1982).

Lindenbaum v. *City of Philadelphia,* 584 F. Supp. 1190 (E.D. Pa. 1984).

Maryland Public Interest Research Group v. *Elkins,* 565 F.2d 864 (4th Cir. 1978); *cert. denied,* 435 U.S. 1008 (1978).

Perry v. *Local Lodge 2569 of the International Association of Machinists and Aerospace Workers,* 708 F.2d 1258 (7th Cir. 1983).

Stanley v. *McGrath,* 719 F.2d 279 (8th Cir. 1983).

Veed v. *Schwartzkopf,* 353 F. Supp. 149 (D. Neb. 1973); *aff'd mem.,* 478 F.2d 1407 (8th Cir. 1973); *cert. denied,* 414 U.S. 1135 (1974).

Commercial speech

American Future Systems v. *Pennsylvania State University,* 464 F. Supp. 1252 (M.D. Pa. 1979); *aff'd,* 618 F.2d 252 (3rd Cir. 1980) [AFS1].

American Future Systems v. *Pennsylvania State University,* 552 F. Supp. 554 (M.D. Pa. 1981); 688 F.2d 907 (3rd Cir. 1982) [AFS2].

American Future Systems v. *Pennsylvania State University,* 553 F. Supp. 1268 (M.D. Pa. 1982); 568 F. Supp. 666 (M.D. Pa. 1983); *rev'd,* 752 F.2d 854 (3rd Cir. 1984); *cert. denied, Johnson* v. *Pennsylvania State University,* 105 S.Ct. 3537 (1985) [AFS3].

Brooks v. *Auburn University*, 412 F.2d 1171 (5th Cir. 1969).

Central Hudson Gas and Electric Corporation v. *Public Service Commission at New York*, 447 U.S. 557 (1980).

Cox v. *Louisiana*, 379 U.S. 536 (1965).

Grayned v. *City of Rockford*, 408 U.S. 104 (1972).

Ohralik v. *Ohio State Bar Association*, 436 U.S. 447 (1978).

Perry Education Association v. *Perry Local Educators Association*, 460 U.S. 37 (1983).

Spartacus Youth League v. *Board of Trustees of Illinois Industrial University*, 502 F. Supp. 789 (N.D. Ill. 1980).

Virginia State Board of Pharmacy v. *Virginia Citizens Consumer Council*, 425 U.S. 748 (1976).

Educational malpractice and academic deference

Bain v. *Gillispie*, 357 N.W.2d 47 (Iowa Ct. App. 1984).

Brown v. *North Carolina Wesleyan College, Inc.*, 309 S.E.2d 701 (N.C. Ct. App. 1983).

Crook v. *Baker*, 584 F. Supp. 1531 (E.D. Mich. 1984).

Donohue v. *Copiague Free School District*, 408 N.Y.S.2d 584 (N.Y. Sup. Ct. 1977); *aff'd*, 407 N.Y.S.2d 874 (N.Y. App. Div. 1978); *aff'd*, 418 N.Y.S.2d 375 (N.Y. 1979).

Ewing v. *Board of Regents of the University of Michigan*, 742 F.2d 913 (6th Cir. 1984), *rev'd*, *Regents of the University of Michigan* v. *Ewing*, 106 S.Ct. 507 (1985).

Greenhill v. *Bailey*, 519 F.2d 5 (8th Cir. 1975).

Hines v. *Rinker*, 667 F.2d 699 (8th Cir. 1981).

Hoffman v. *Board of Education of the City of New York*, 410 N.Y.S.2d 99 (N.Y. App. Div. 1978); *rev'd*, 424 N.Y.S.2d 376 (N.Y. 1979).

Jones v. *Board of Governors of University of North Carolina*, 704 F.2d 713 (4th Cir. 1983).

Miller v. *State*, 478 N.Y.S.2d 829 (N.Y. 1984).

Moore v. *Vanderloo*, 386 N.W.2d 108 (Iowa 1986).

Neel v. *I.U. Board of Trustees*, 435 N.E.2d 607 (Ind. Ct. App. 1982).

Pape v. *State*, 456 N.Y.S.2d 863 (N.Y. App. Div. 1983).

Patti Ann H. v. *New York Medical College*, 453 N.Y.S.2d 196 (N.Y. 1982).

Peter W. v. *San Francisco Unified School District*, 131 Cal. Rptr. 854 (Cal. Ct. App. 1976).

Peterson v. *San Francisco Community College District*, 685 P.2d 1193 (Cal. 1984).

Sipple v. *Board of Governors of the University of North Carolina*, 318 S.E.2d 256 (N.C. Ct. App. 1984).

Swidryk v. *St. Michael's Medical Center*, 493 A.2d 641 (N.J. Super. Ct. Law Div. 1985).

Van Stry v. *State*, 479 N.Y.S.2d 258 (N.Y. App. Div. 1984).

Woodruff v. *Georgia State University*, 304 S.E.2d 697 (Ga. 1983).

INDEX

Bonner (see *Gay Students Organization of the University of New Hampshire* v. *Bonner)*

Brooks v. *Auburn University,* 41

Brown v. *North Carolina Wesleyan College,* 52

Buckley Amendment, 13

Burden of proof, 64

Buttney v. *Smiley,* 2, 14

C

California State Universities and Colleges (see *Associated Students, San Jose State University* v. *Trustees of California State Universities and Colleges)*

Campus facilities, 17–28

Campus post office box use, 18

Carr v. *St. Johns University,* 3

Central Connecticut State College, 17

Central Hudson Gas and Electric Corporation v. *Public Service Commission at New York,* 42, 45

Central Missouri State College (see *Estaban* v. *Central Missouri State College)*

Cheating, 11, 12, 59, 64

Check-off system (fees), 34, 39, 66

Church-state separation, 28

Civil rights demonstrations, 5

Code of fair practice, 4

Colorado State Board of Agriculture (see *Evans* v. *State Board of Agriculture)*

Commercial speech
    case law, 42–43
    First Amendment protection, 41
    on campus, 43–45
    outside residence rooms, 45–46
    policy considerations, 66–67
    regulations, 46–47

Committee on Gay Education (University of Georgia), 25

Concerts: student fees for, 32

Connecticut (see *Griswold* v. *Connecticut)*

Constitutional rights, 1, 63–64

Consumerism, 4, 60

Contract theory
    educational malpractice, 49, 50, 52–53
    public and private colleges, 17, 50, 53
    student-institution relationship, 3–5

"Contract to educate," 4

Copiague Free School District (see *Donohue* v. *Copiague Free School District)*

Cornerstone, 22, 23

F

Faculty evaluation process, 67
Fair practice, 4
Family Educational Rights and Privacy Act of 1974, 13
Federal regulation, 13–14
Fees (see Activity fees)
Fiduciary relationship, 3
Fifth Amendment, 12
Financial aid, 13
First Amendment (see also Freedom of assembly; Freedom of association; Freedom of speech; Freedom of the press), 1, 6, 12, 17, 21, 24, 32, 33, 35, 36, 41, 63, 64–67
"Foreseeable risk," 51, 52
Fourteenth Amendment, 5, 7, 17, 20, 63, 64
Fourth Amendment, 12
Fraud theory, 50
Freedom of assembly, 14, 64
Freedom of association, 14, 16, 17–28, 29, 30, 64
Freedom of press, 5, 14
Freedom of religion (see Religion)
Freedom of speech, 5, 14–16, 18, 20, 22, 23, 41–47, 64, 65

G

Galda v. *Rutgers*, 36–39
Gay Activists Alliance v. *Board of Regents of University of Oklahoma*, 25
Gay Liberation v. *University of Missouri*, 16
Gay Rights Coalition v. *Georgetown University*, 26–27
Gay Student Services v. *Texas A&M University*, 24
Gay Students Organization of the University of New Hampshire v. *Bonner*, 16, 19
Gay student organizations, 23–27
Georgetown University (see *Gay Rights Coalition* v. *Georgetown University*)
Georgia State University (see *Woodruff* v. *Georgia State University*)
Good v. *Associated Students, University of Washington*, 32
Gott v. *Berea College*, 2
Grades/qualifications (see also Academic deference), 59
Grayned v. *City of Rockford*, 21, 42
Greenhill v. *Bailey*, 59
Griswold v. *Connecticut*, 12
Gross v. *Lopez*, 9
Grove City College v. *Bell*, 13
Guest speakers, 32

H

Hammond v. *South Carolina State College,* 15
Handicapped
    discrimination prevention, 13, 14
    wrongful identification, 55–56
Health issues: student fees, 32
Healy v. *James,* 14, 15, 16, 17, 18, 19, 25, 27
Healy v. *Larsson,* 4
Hearing
    requirement, 8
    suspension before, 9
Henson v. *Honor Committee of the University of Virginia,*
    9, 10, 63
High school graduation: malpractice, 53
Hines v. *Rinker,* 59
Hockey: physical injury, 51
Hoffman v. *Board of Education of the City of New York,* 55, 56
Homosexual rights, 16, 23–27
Honor codes (see *Henson* v. *Honor Committee of the University*
    of Virginia)
Horowitz (see *Board of Curators of the University of Missouri* v.
    Horowitz)
Human-Rights Act of 1977 (Washington, D.C.), 26

I

Illinois Industrial University (see *Spartacus Youth League* v.
    Board of Trustees of Illinois Industrial University)
Implied contract, 4
In loco parentis
    basis for student-college relationship, 1, 5
    case law, 1–3
Indiana University (see *Neel* v. *I. U. Board of Trustees*)
Individual rights, 7–8, 13–14
Injuries: physical, 50–52
International Association of Machinists and Aerospace Workers
    (see *Perry* v. *Local 2569 of the International Association of*
    Machinists and Aerospace Workers)

J

Jenkins v. *Louisiana State Board of Education,* 9
Jones v. *Board of Governors of University of North Carolina,* 59
Judicial deference to academicians, 58–60

K

Kentucky Educators Public Affairs Council v. *Kentucky Registry*
    of Election Finance, 35

L

Liability
　　contract, 52–53
　　physical injury, 50–52
Lindenbaum v. *City of Philadelphia,* 30
Litigation evolution, 63
Lobbying groups, 36
Locker room injury, 51
Louisiana State Board of Education (see *Jenkins* v. *Louisiana State Board of Education)*

M

Mail service: solicitation, 43, 44, 45, 67
Malpractice
　　education 53–56
　　in higher education, 56–57
　　literature on, 57–58
　　policy, 67–68
　　theory, 49–50
Mandatory fees, 29–39
Maryland Public Interest Research Group v. *Elkins,* 31
Medical education
　　educational malpractice, 57
　　student dismissal, 11
Miller v. *State,* 51
Moore v. *Student Affairs Committee of Troy State University,* 2, 12
Moore v. *Vanderloo,* 57

N

Neel v. *I. U. Board of Trustees,* 59
Negligence, 51, 53, 54
Newspapers
　　commercial speech mechanism, 43, 44, 45, 46, 47, 67
　　prior restraint, 15
　　student activity fees for, 32, 35
New Jersey Public Interest Research Group, 36–39
New York City Board of Education (see *Hoffman* v. *Board of Education of the City of New York)*
New York Medical College (see *Patti Ann H.* v. *New York Medical College)*
New York State (see *Pape* v. *State; Van Stry* v. *State)*
New York State Education Commission (see *Steier* v. *New York State Education Commission)*
Nittany Lion Inn, 45
Noncommercial speech, 41–42

Privacy
    residence hall solicitation, 44
    search and seizure, 12–13
    student rights, 63
Private institutions
    contractual relationships, 4, 17, 50, 53
    ethical precedents, 7
    gay student organizations, 26–27
Public forum doctrine, 20, 21
Public Interest Research Group (PIRG), 31, 36–39
Public institutions
    academic dismissal, 59
    contract theory, 53
    due process requirement, 1, 8
    First Amendment boundaries, 14–16, 17, 18
    Fourteenth Amendment protection, 5, 7, 17, 63
    recognition of organizations/facility use, 64–65
    religious organizations, 21–23
    state vs. federal jurisdiction, 5
Public policy argument, 54, 56, 57, 58
Publications (see also Newspapers)
    editorial content protection, 64
    limited guarantees, 67
    organizational recognition, 19

R
Radio, 43, 44, 45, 46, 47, 67
Rape, 51, 52
Recognition of organizations, 17–20, 23–27, 64–65
Recruitment, 13
Refunds (fees), 34, 37, 38
Regents of the University of Michigan v. *Ewing* (see also *Ewing*
    v. *Board of Regents of the University of Michigan*), 11, 60
Rehabilitation Act of 1973, 13
Religion
    freedom of, 22, 27, 31
    objections to activity fees, 31–32
    organizations, 21–23
Residence halls
    commercial solicitation in, 43, 44, 66–67
    privacy, 63
    rape, 52
    search and seizure, 12, 13
Reverse check-off system (fees), 34, 39, 66
Right to counsel, 10
Right to post notices, 19
Rock groups: student fees for, 32
Rutgers University (see *Galda* v. *Rutgers*)

S

Salespeople, 43
San Francisco Community College District (see *Peterson* v. *San Francisco Community College District)*
San Francisco Unified School District (see *Peter W.* v. *San Francisco Unified School District)*
San Jose State University (see *Associated Students, San Jose State University* v. *Trustees of California State Universities and Colleges)*
School name/media use, 18, 19
SDS (see Students for a Democratic Society)
Search and seizure, 12
Separation of church and state, 28
Sipple v. *Board of Governors of the University of North Carolina,* 52
Solicitation, 41–47, 66–67
South Carolina State College (see *Hammond* v. *South Carolina State College)*
Southeastern Community College v. *Davis,* 14
Spartacus Youth League v. *Board of Trustees of Illinois Industrial University,* 45
Speakers: protection of, 32, 64
Speakes v. *Grantham,* 12
Speech (see Freedom of speech)
St. Johns University (see *Carr* v. *St. Johns University)*
St. Michael's Medical Center (see *Swidryk* v. *St. Michael's Medical Center)*
Stacy v. *Williams,* 15
Standard of care: teachers, 54, 57, 58
Standard of proof, 10
Stanley v. *McGrath,* 35, 36
Steier v. *New York State Education Commission,* 5
Student activity funds, 18
Student affairs administrators
    disciplinary procedures, 10
    educational malpractice, 49
    search and seizure, 12
Student Coalition for Gay Rights v. *Austin Peay State University,* 24
Student fees (see Activity fees)
Student government associations, 30–31, 32, 33
Student handbooks, 19
Student organizations
    gay students, 23–27
    group rights, 6
    off-campus, 36–38

Troy State University (see *Moore* v. *Student Affairs Committee of Troy State University*)
"Trust theory," 3

U
Union dues, 29–30
University of California (see *Erzinger* v. *Regents of the University of California*)
University of Georgia, 25
University of Michigan (see *Ewing* v. *Board of Regents of the University of Michigan; Regents of the University of Michigan* v. *Ewing*)
University of Missouri (see *Board of Curators of the University of Missouri* v. *Horowitz; Gay Liberation* v. *University of Missouri; Papish* v. *Board of Curators of the University of Missouri*)
University of Missouri at Kansas City, 22
University of New Hampshire (see *Gay Students Organization of the University of New Hampshire* v. *Bonner*)
University of North Carolina (see *Jones* v. *Board of Governors of University of North Carolina; Sipple* v. *Board of Governors of the University of North Carolina*)
University of Oklahoma (see *Gay Activists Alliance* v. *Board of Regents of University of of Oklahoma*)
University of Virginia (see *Henson* v. *Honor Committee of the University of Virginia*)
University of Washington (see *Good* v. *Associated Students, University of Washington*)

V
Van Stry v. *State*, 51
Veed v. *Schwartzkopf*, 32, 33
Vendors: access to campus, 45–47, 67
Vietnam War protest, 1
Violation of state/federal law, 25, 65
Violence potential, 25, 27, 64, 65
Virginia State Board of Pharmacy v. *Virginia Citizens Consumer Council*, 42

W
Widmar v. *Vincent*, 22, 23
Wood v. *Davison*, 25, 26
Woodruff v. *Georgia State University*, 59
Worship (see Religion)
Wright v. *Texas Southern University*, 9
Written notice, 9, 11

ASHE-ERIC HIGHER EDUCATION REPORTS

Starting in 1983, the Association for the Study of Higher Education assumed cosponsorship of the Higher Education Reports with the ERIC Clearinghouse on Higher Education. For the previous 11 years, ERIC and the American Association for Higher Education prepared and published the reports.

Each report is the definitive analysis of a tough higher education problem, based on a thorough research of pertinent literature and institutional experiences. Report topics, identified by a national survey, are written by noted practitioners and scholars with prepublication manuscript reviews by experts.

Eight monographs (10 monographs before 1985) in the ASHE-ERIC Higher Education Report series are published each year, available individually or by subscription. Subscription to eight issues is $60 regular; $50 for members of AERA, AAHE, and AIR; $40 for members of ASHE. (Add $7.50 outside the United States.)

Prices for single copies, including 4th class postage and handling, are $10.00 regular and $7.50 for members of AERA, AAHE, AIR, and ASHE ($7.50 regular and $6.00 for members for 1983 and 1984 reports, $6.50 regular and $5.00 for members for reports published before 1983). If faster 1st class postage is desired for U.S. and Canadian orders, add $.75 for each publication ordered; overseas, add $4.50. For VISA and MasterCard payments, include card number, expiration date, and signature. Orders under $25 must be prepaid. Bulk discounts are available on orders of 15 or more reports (not applicable to subscriptions). Order from the Publications Department, Association for the Study of Higher Education, One Dupont Circle, Suite 630, Washington, D.C. 20036, 202/296-2597. Write for a publication list of all the Higher Education Reports available.

1986 Higher Education Reports

1. Post-tenure Faculty Evaluation: Threat or Opportunity?
   Christine M. Licata
2. Blue Ribbon Commissions and Higher Education: Changing Academe from the Outside
   Janet R. Johnson and Laurence R. Marcus
3. Responsive Professional Education: Balancing Outcomes and Opportunities
   Joan S. Stark, Malcolm A. Lowther, and Bonnie M.K. Hagerty
4. Increasing Students' Learning: A Faculty Guide to Reducing Stress among Students
   Neal A. Whitman, David C. Spendlove, and Claire H. Clark
5. Student Financial Aid and Women: Equity Dilemma?
   Mary Moran
6. The Master's Degree: Tradition, Diversity, Innovation
   Judith S. Glazer
7. The College, the Constitution, and the Consumer Student: Implications for Policy and Practice
   Robert M. Hendrickson and Annette Gibbs

1985 Higher Education Reports

1. Flexibility in Academic Staffing: Effective Policies and Practices
   Kenneth P. Mortimer, Marque Bagshaw, and Andrew T. Masland

---

10. Faculty Workload: Research, Theory, and Interpretation
    Harold E. Yuker

1983 Higher Education Reports

1. The Path to Excellence: Quality Assurance in Higher Education
   Laurence R. Marcus, Anita O. Leone, and Edward D. Goldberg

2. Faculty Recruitment, Retention, and Fair Employment: Obligations
   and Opportunities
   John S. Waggaman

3. Meeting the Challenges: Developing Faculty Careers
   Michael C. T. Brookes and Katherine L. German

4. Raising Academic Standards: A Guide to Learning Improvement
   Ruth Talbott Keimig

5. Serving Learners at a Distance: A Guide to Program Practices
   Charles E. Feasley

6. Competence, Admissions, and Articulation: Returning to the Basics
   in Higher Education
   Jean L. Preer

7. Public Service in Higher Education: Practices and Priorities
   Patricia H. Crosson

8. Academic Employment and Retrenchment: Judicial Review and
   Administrative Action
   Robert M. Hendrickson and Barbara A. Lee

9. Burnout: The New Academic Disease
   Winifred Albizu Meléndez and Rafael M. de Guzmán

10. Academic Workplace: New Demands, Heightened Tensions
    Ann E. Austin and Zelda F. Gamson